DOGS are BETTER than CATS

by Missy Dizick & Mary Bly

A Dolphin Book
Doubleday & Company, Inc.
Garden City, New York
1985

A Dolphin Book
Library of Congress Cataloging in Publication Data
Dizick, Missy Camp.
   Dogs are better than cats!
   1. Dogs—Caricatures and cartoons.   2. American wit
and humor, Pictorial.   I. Bly, Mary.   II. Title.
NC1429.D55A4 1985   741.5'973   83-25506
Copyright © 1985 by Missy Dizick and Mary Bly
ISBN: 0-385-19212-6

To Jinx Hone

With thanks to our four-footed research assistants: Molly Bloom, Jasper, Cynthia, Cuckoo, Belle, Ralph, Daphne, Rabbit, Blanche, Eddie, Iving, Fatty Princess, Mandy-Rice, Mrs. Wanda H. Dizick, Simone and Shoestore, Sadie, Bob Whiskers, Froggy, Waylon and Willie, Chloe, Cleo, Lord Plushbottom, Carlos, Gina, Zelda, Bubbles, Percy, Harry McFadden, Centerpiece, Chamaco, Wolfgang, Annie, and Smutt.

Toke ("The Best Dog in the World"), Chena, Pojke, Kootie, Fritz, Tuffy, Rinny, Wosha, Winfield, Laurel, Kitty Carlisle, Megan, Patience, Sarah, Annie, Polly, Foggy, Tubby, Cuddles, Inu, Port and Starboard.

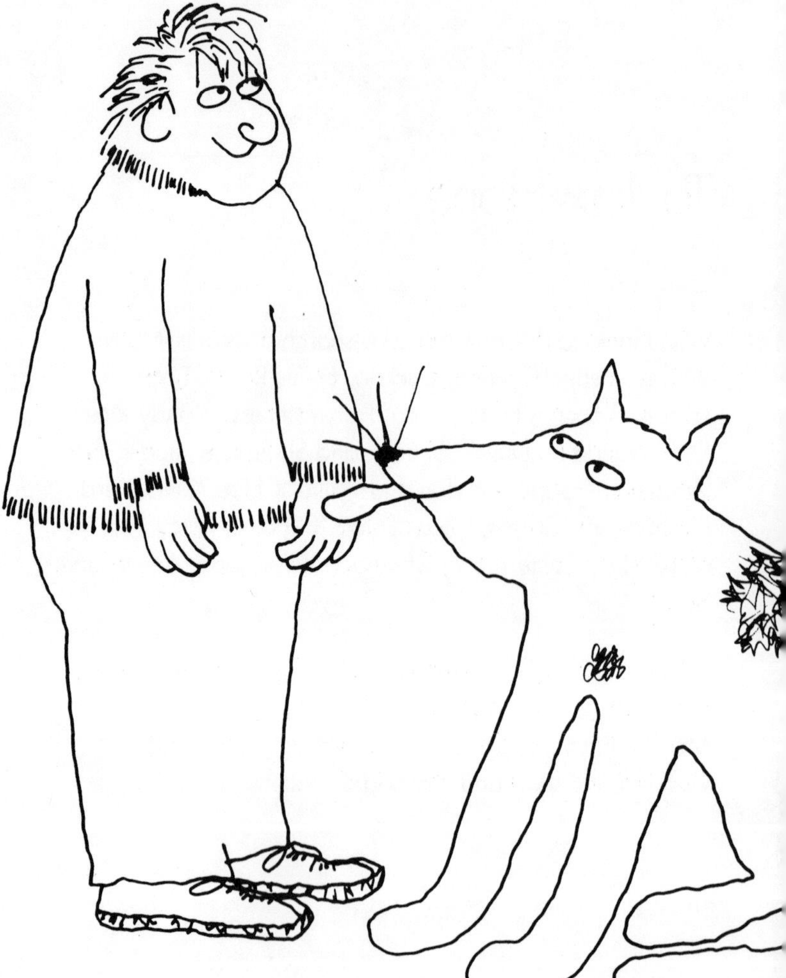

Your DOG loves you.

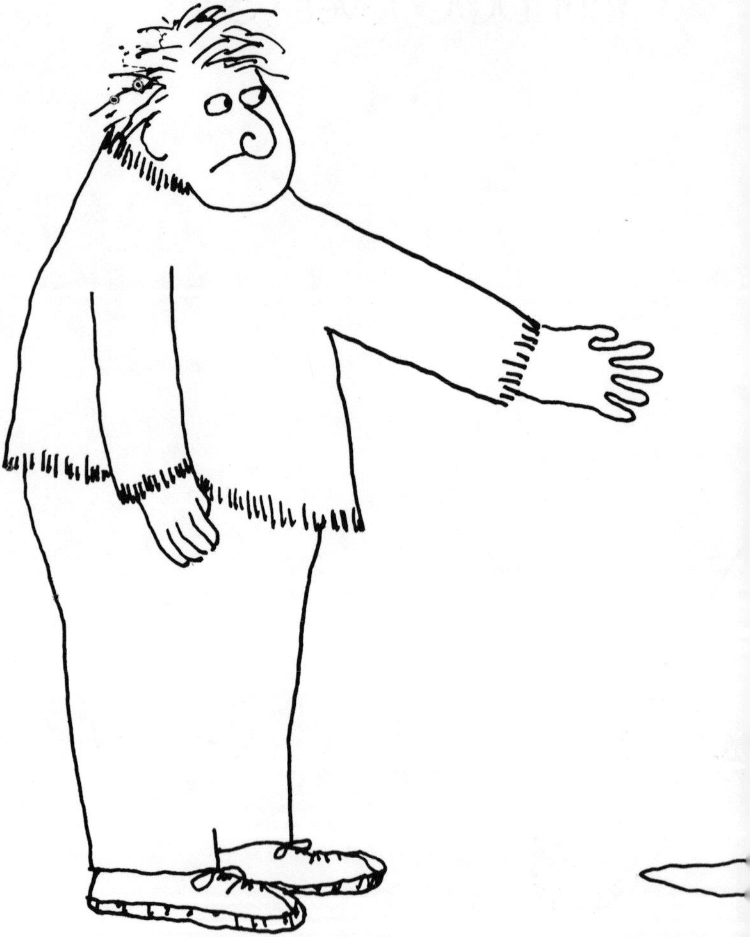

Your CAT thinks you are funny.

DOGS are sincere.

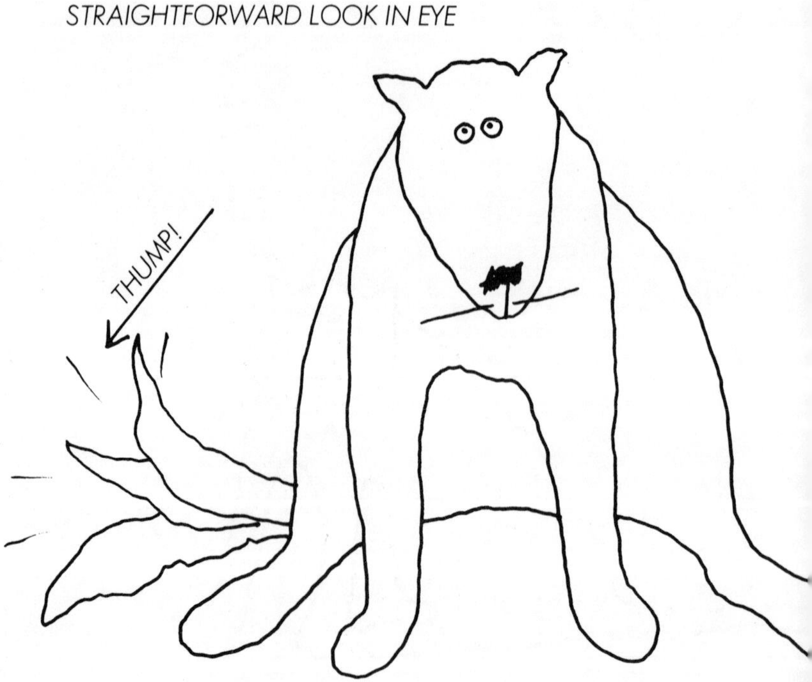
STRAIGHTFORWARD LOOK IN EYE
THUMP!

CATS are sneaky.

DOGS appreciate.

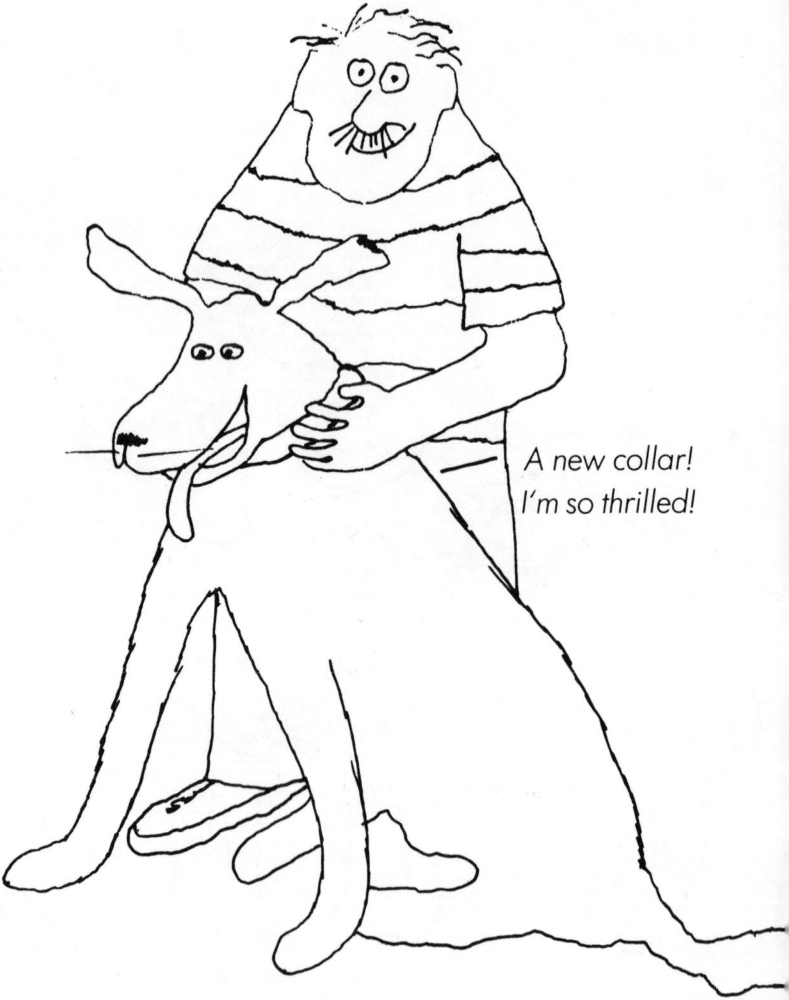
A new collar!
I'm so thrilled!

CATS expect.

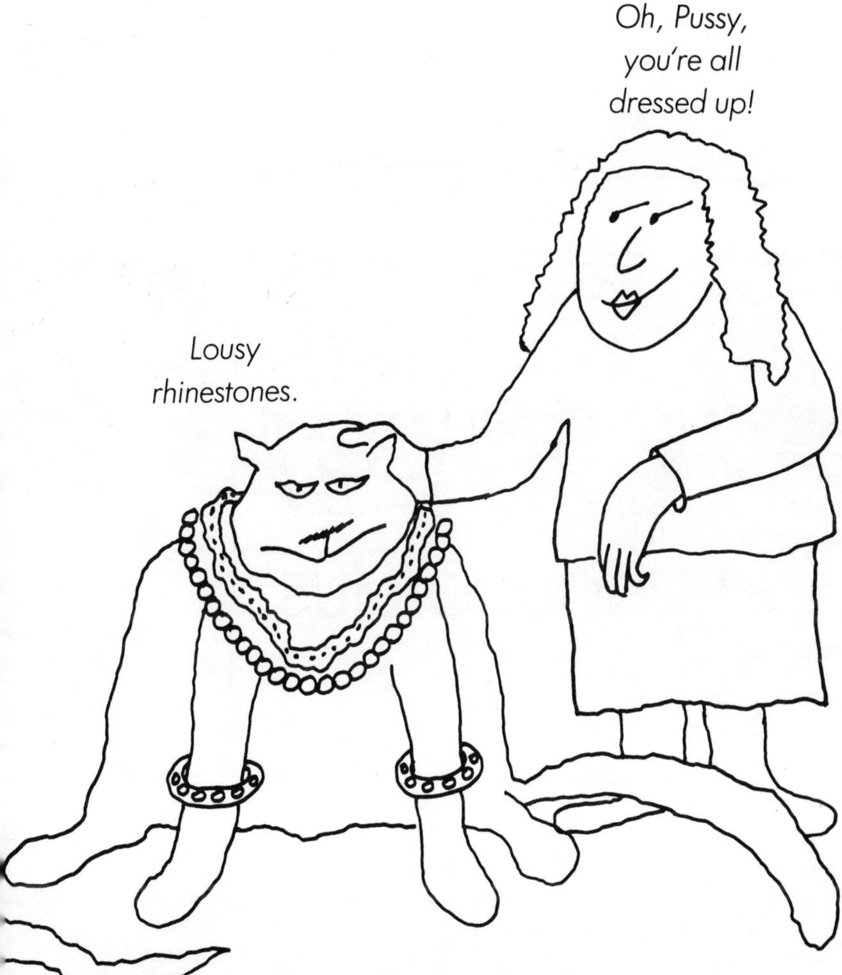
Oh, Pussy,
you're all
dressed up!
Lousy
rhinestones.

DOGS go to school, where they learn *many* useful things.

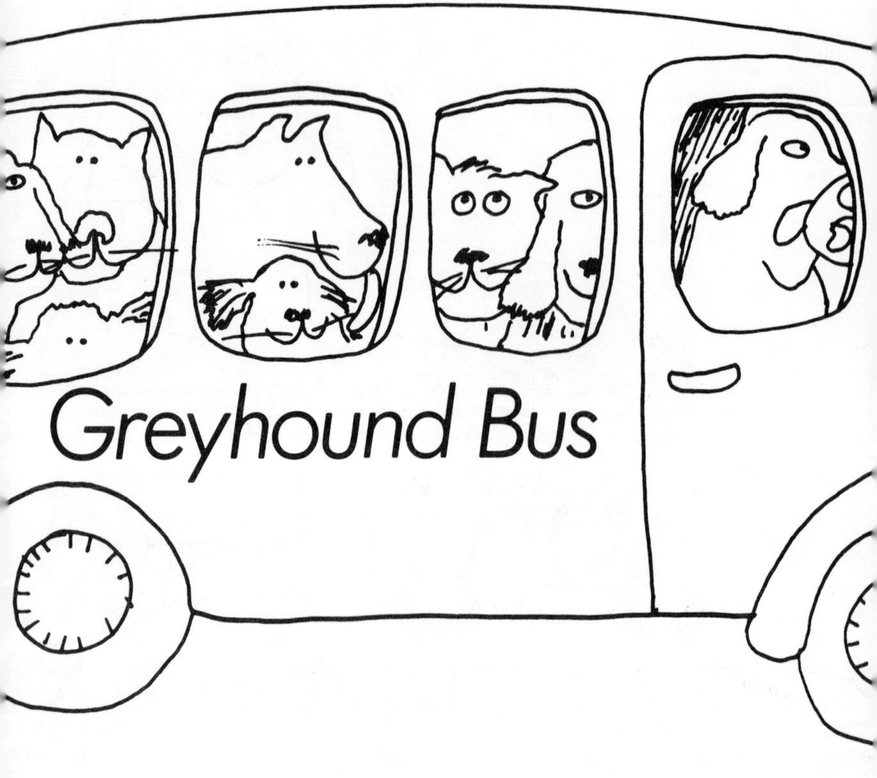
Greyhound Bus

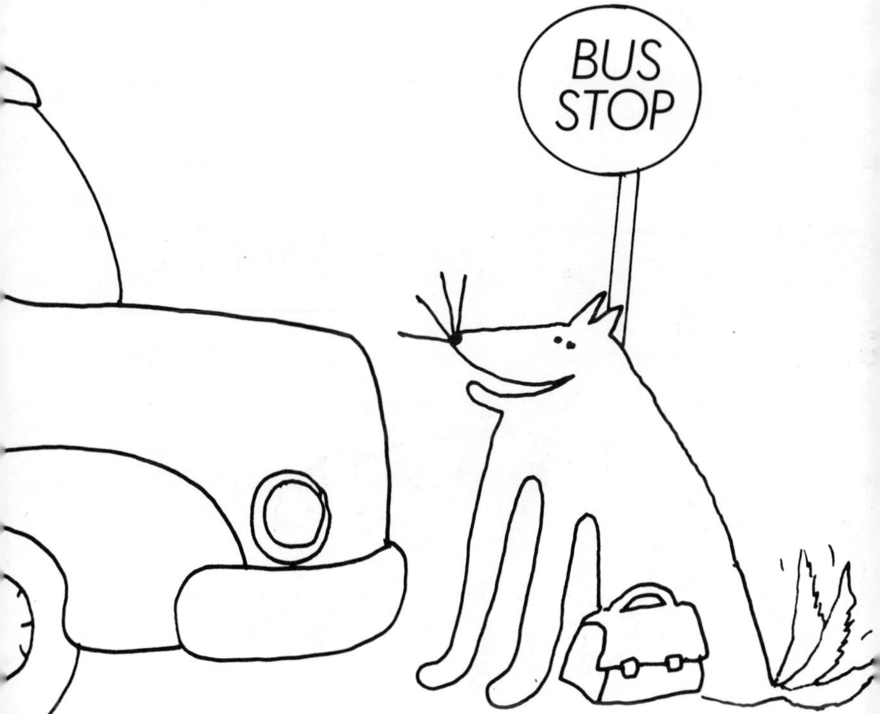
BUS
STOP

But there are NO schools for CATS!

Oh, how swell! Be fat and lazy—
Drive them stupid canines crazy!
Eat good stuff off silver spoon,
Play all night and sleep till noon!

Singing DOGS.

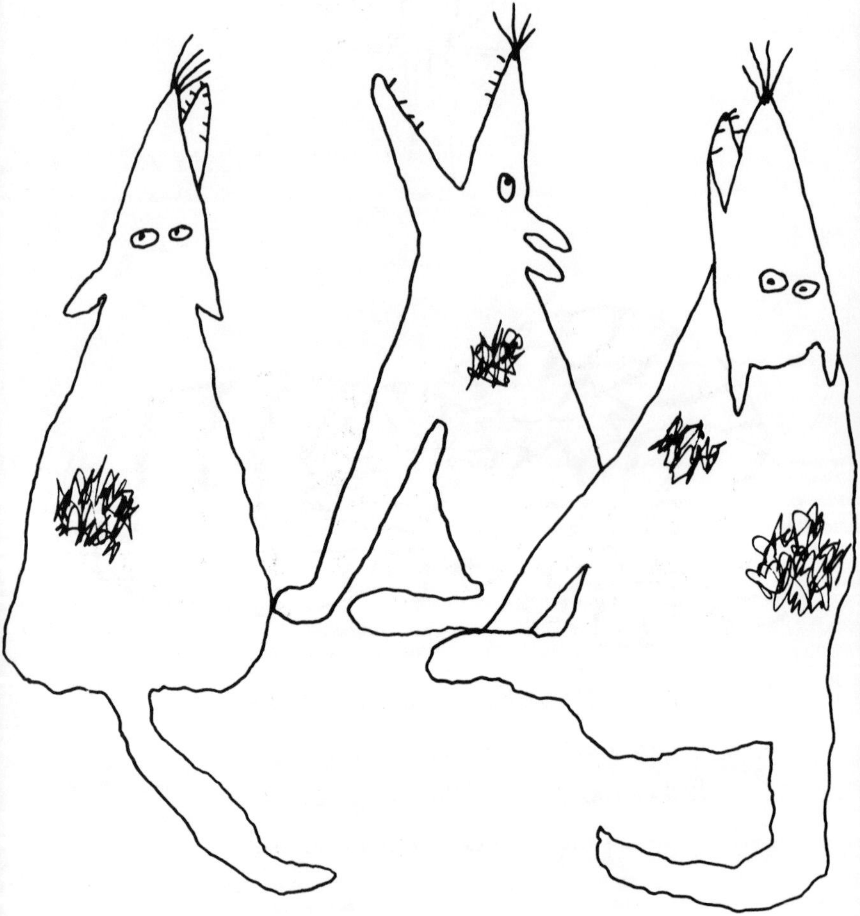

CATerwauling.

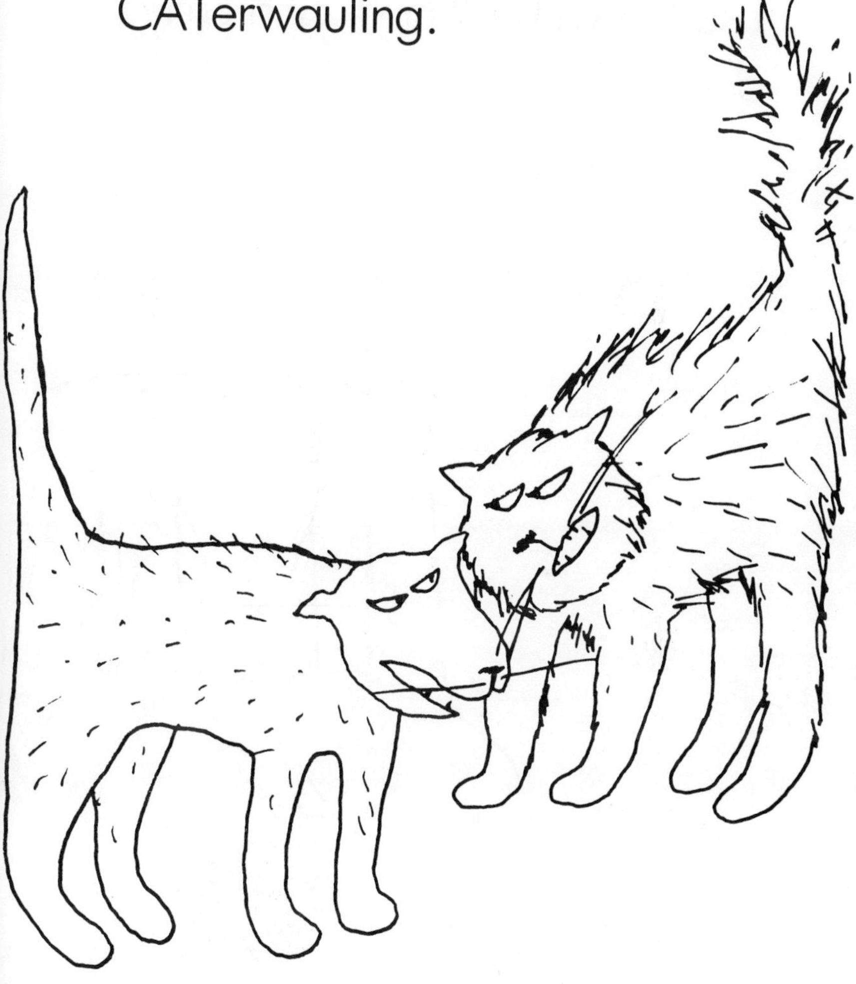

DOGS will roll over and play
dead.

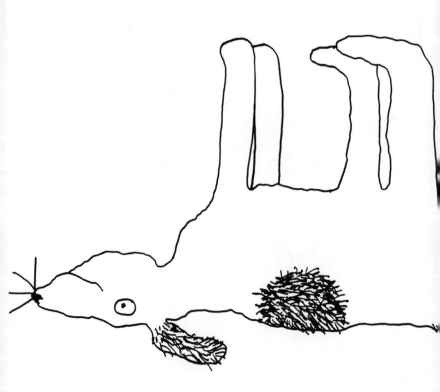

This is a CAT's natural position.

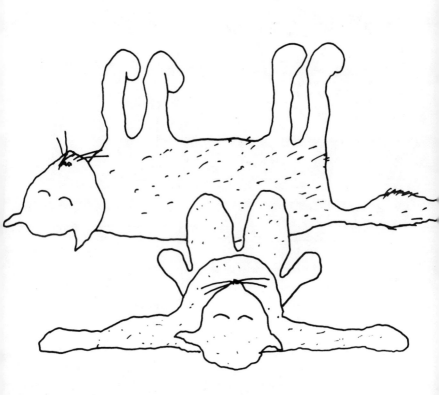

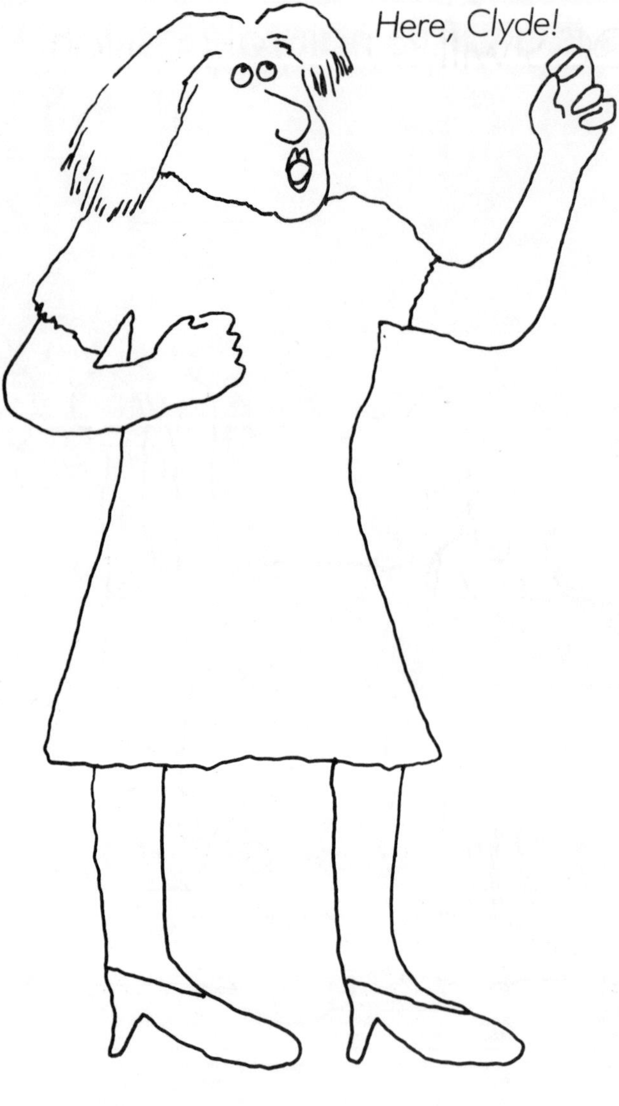
Here, Clyde!

DOGS will come when called.

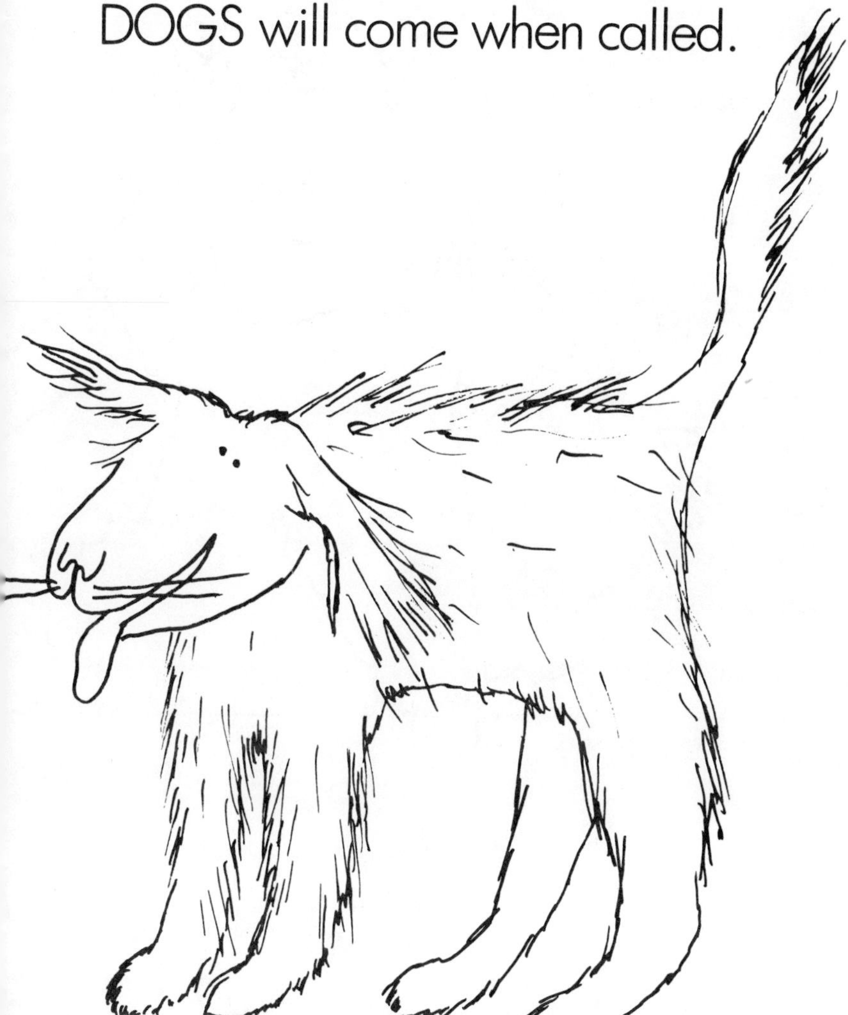

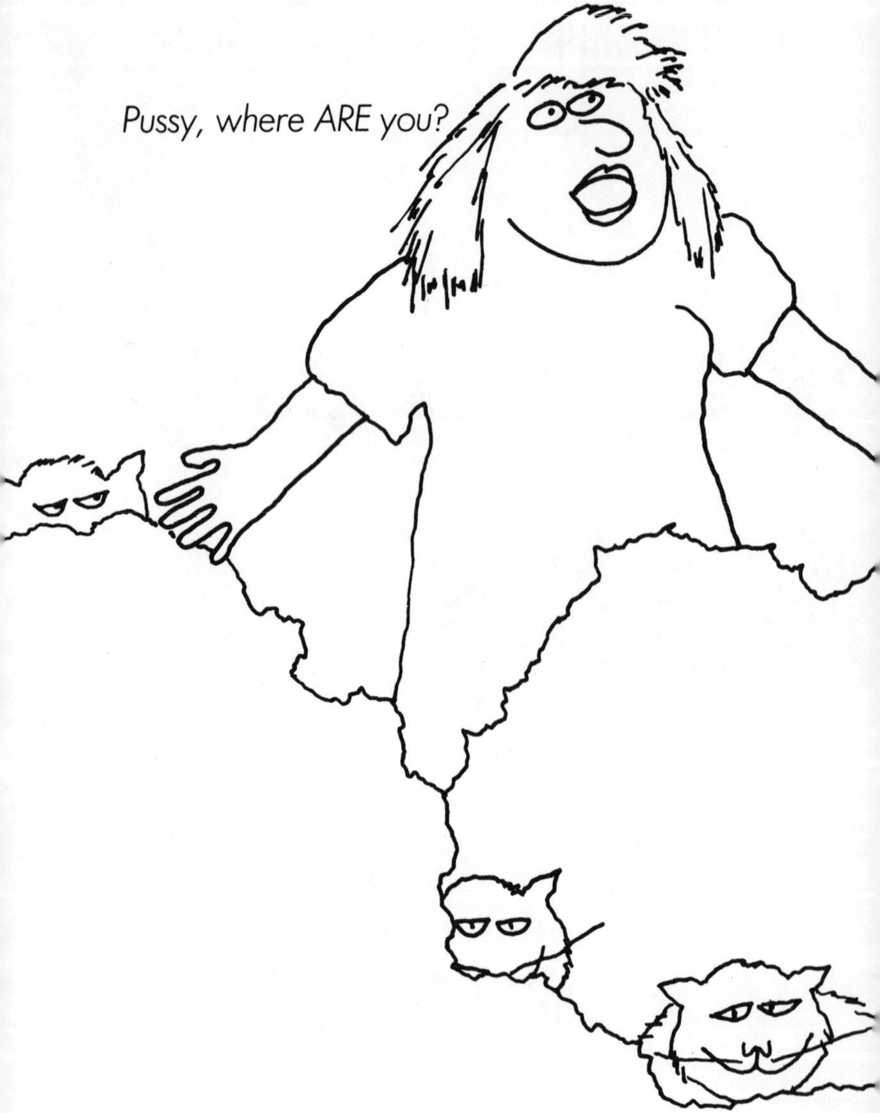
Pussy, where ARE you?

CATS will take a message and get back to you.

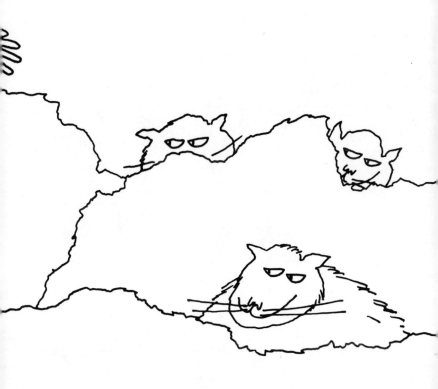

DOGS EAT!

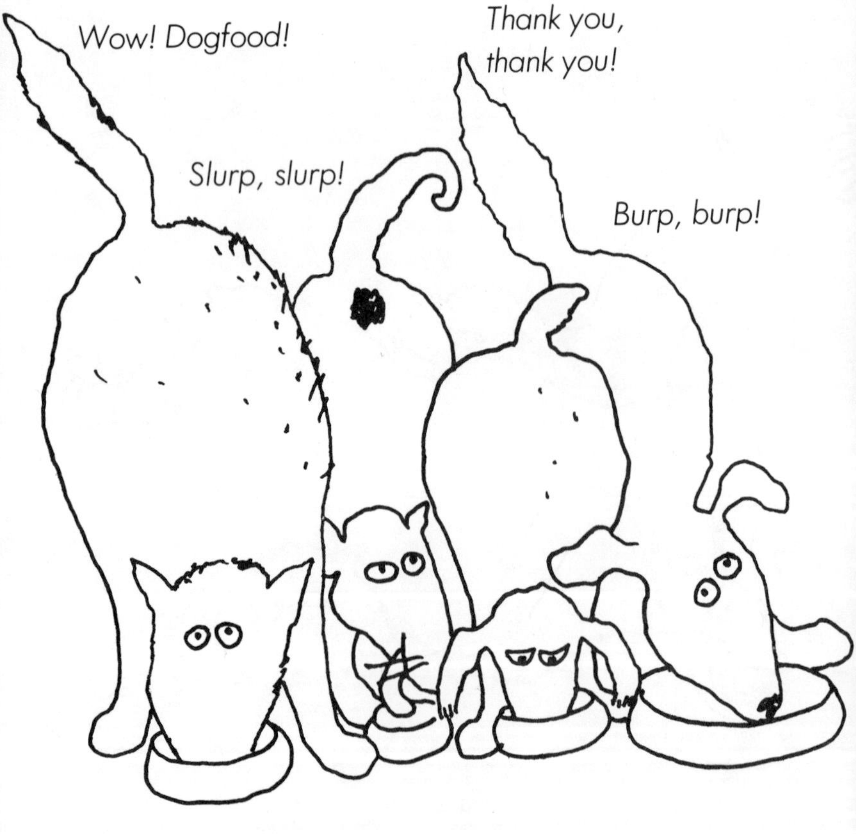

Wow! Dogfood!
Thank you,
thank you!
Slurp, slurp!
Burp, burp!

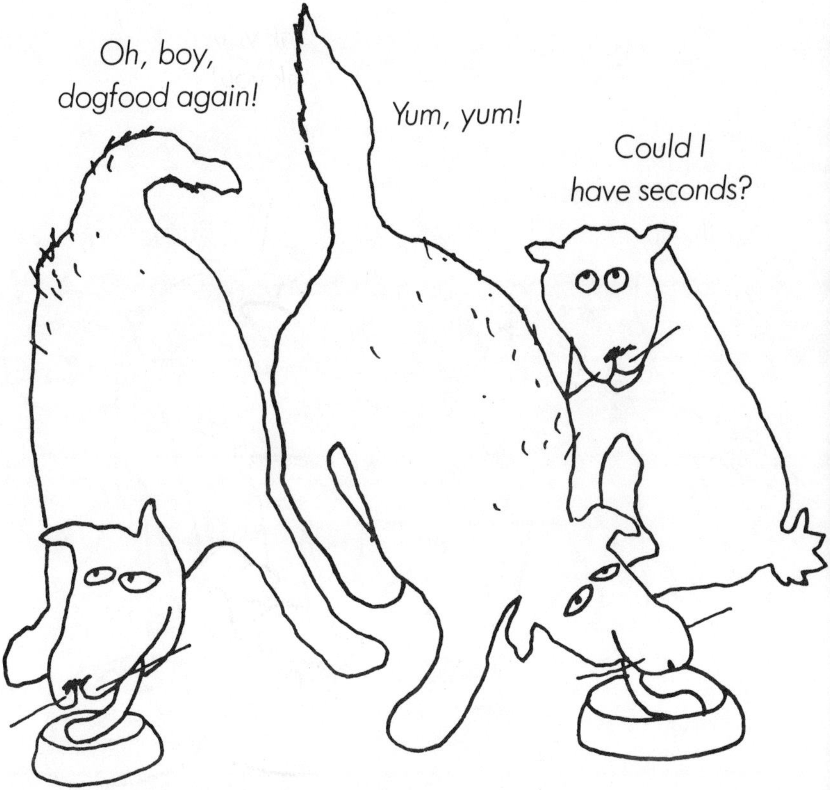
Oh, boy,
dogfood again!
Yum, yum!
Could I
have seconds?

CATS have catered food.

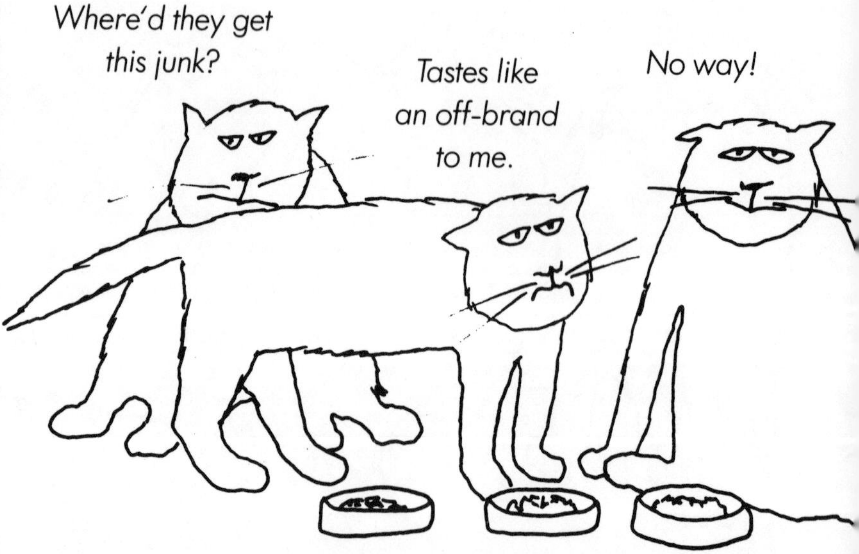
Where'd they get this junk?
Tastes like an off-brand to me.
No way!

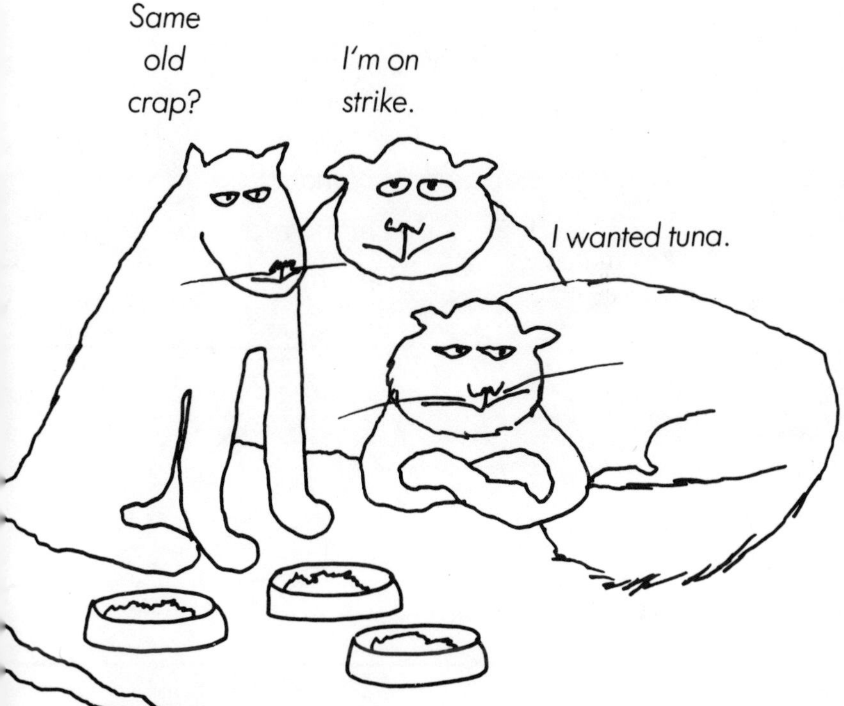

Same old crap?
I'm on strike.
I wanted tuna.

DOGS often own their own homes.

A humble cottage,
but mine own.

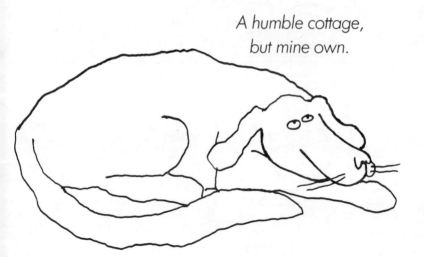

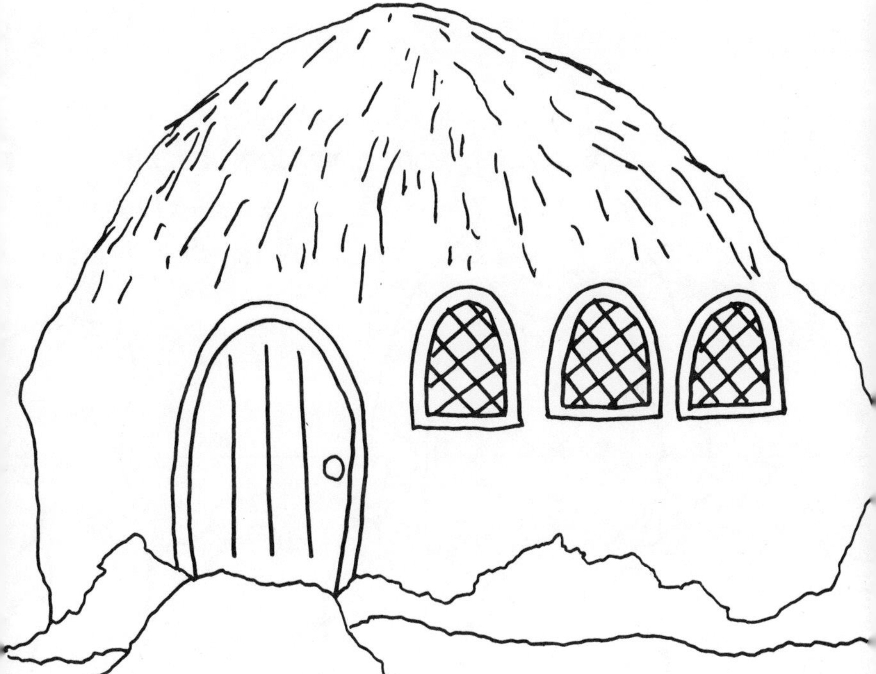

CATS always want to take over yours.

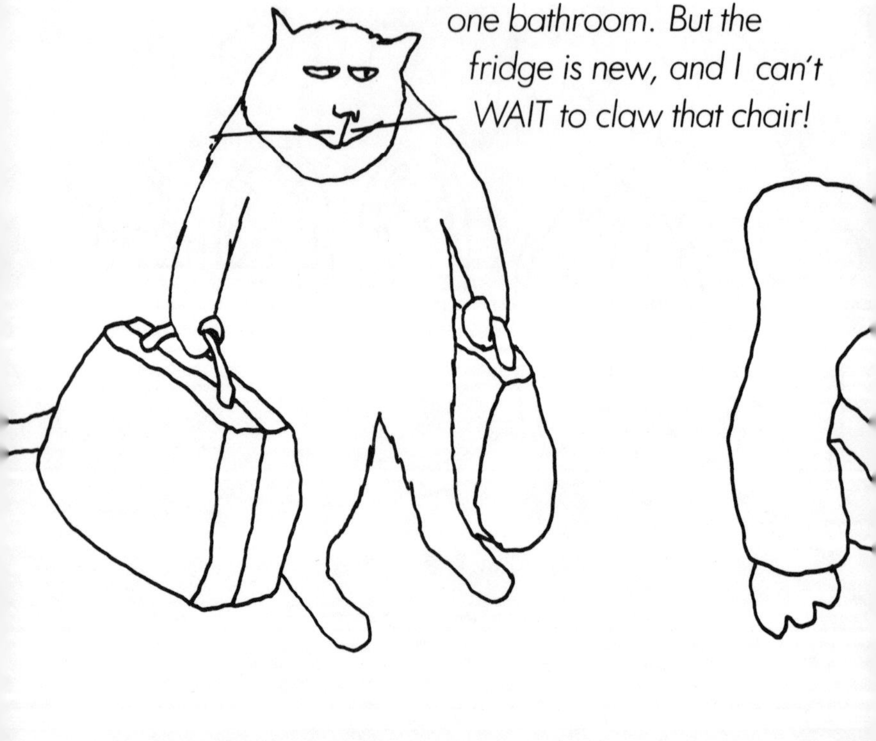
Black and white TV —only one bathroom. But the fridge is new, and I can't WAIT to claw that chair!

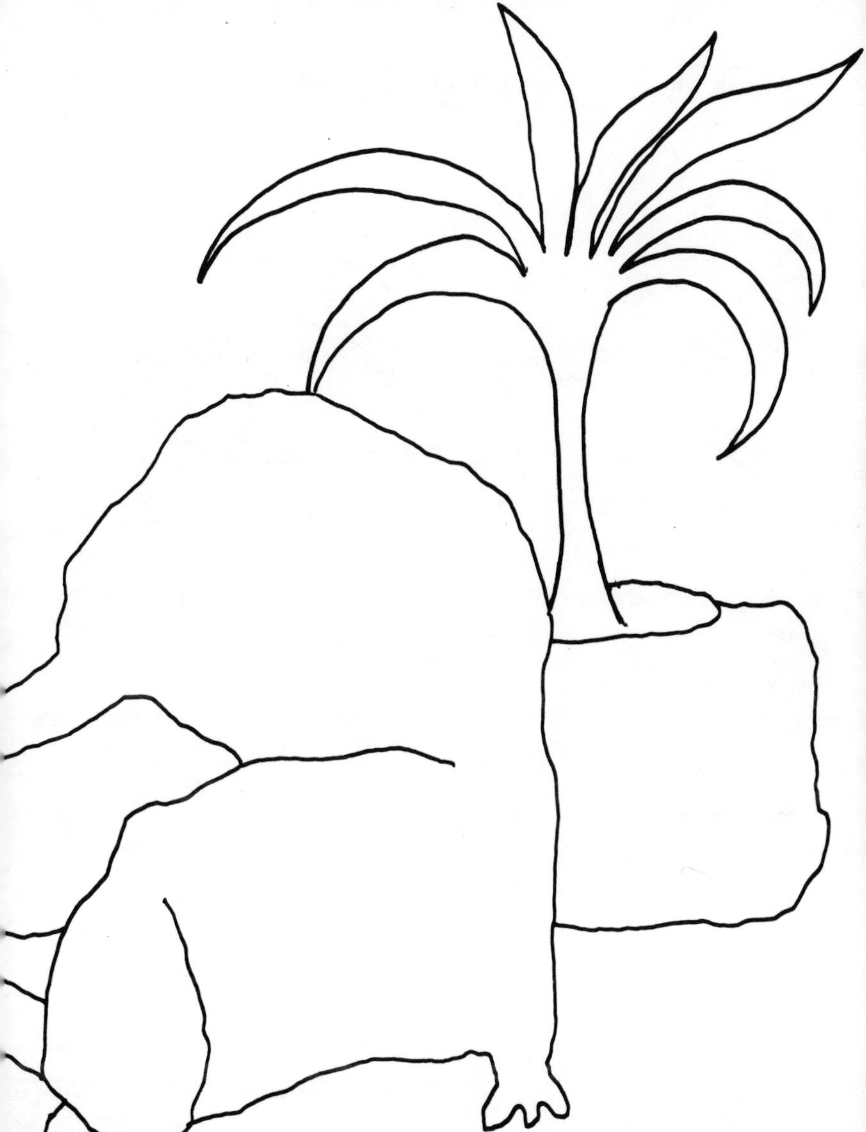

DOGS are trustworthy.

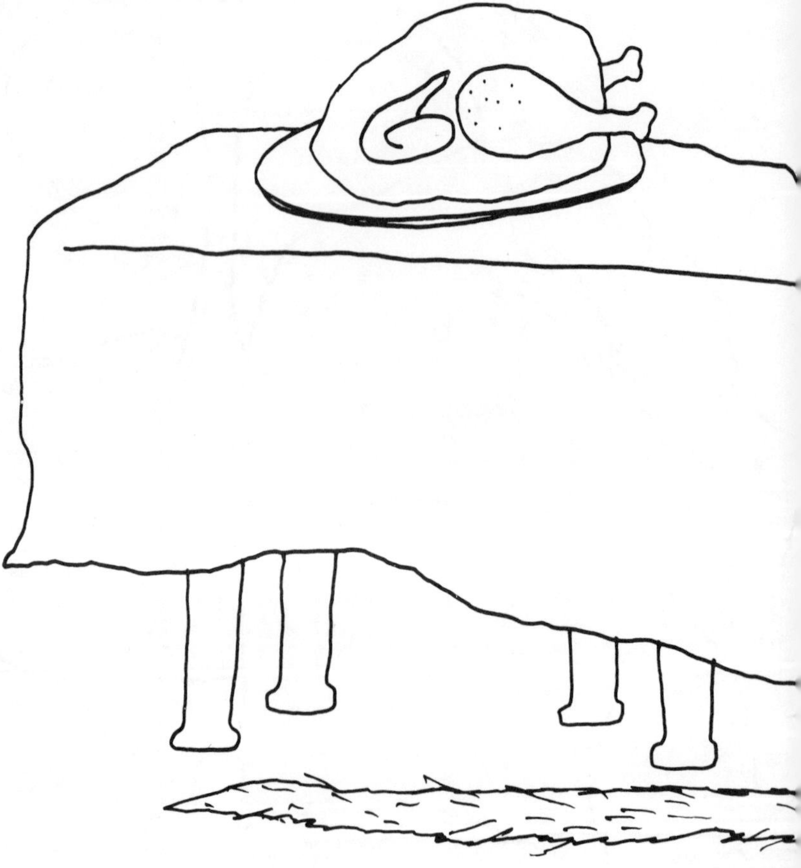

I won't,
I won't!
I won't!

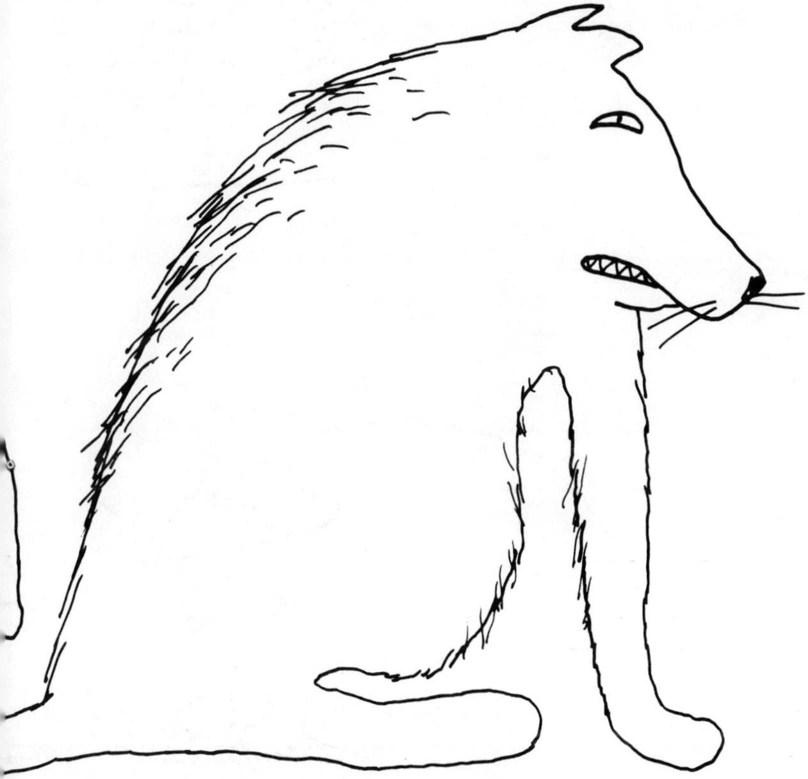

CATS inspired the phrase
"cat burglar."

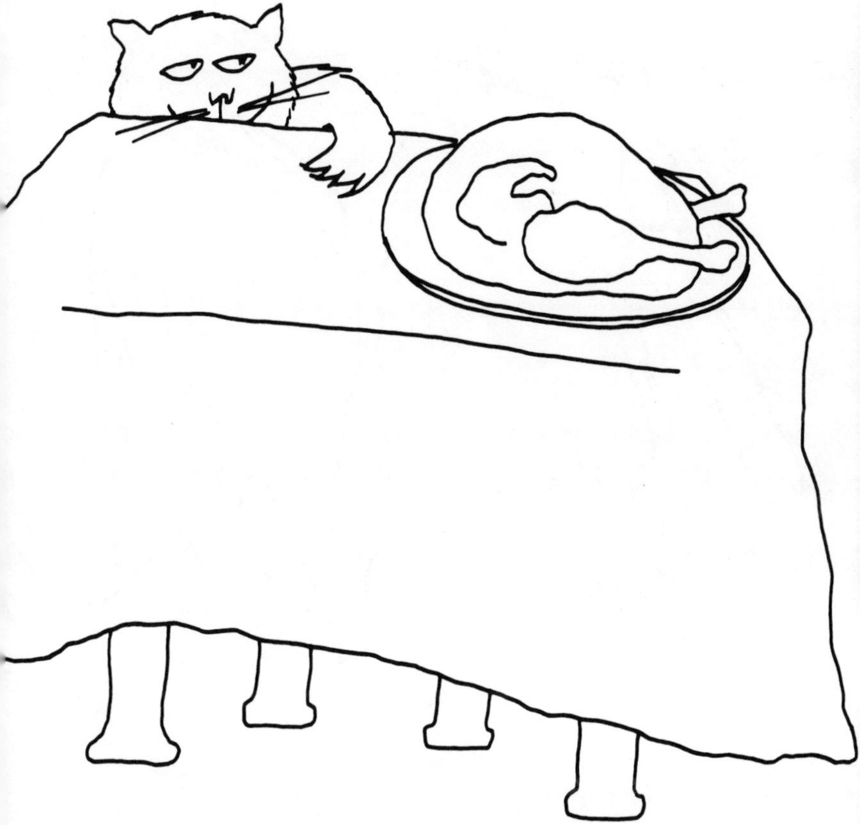

DOGS are high on life.

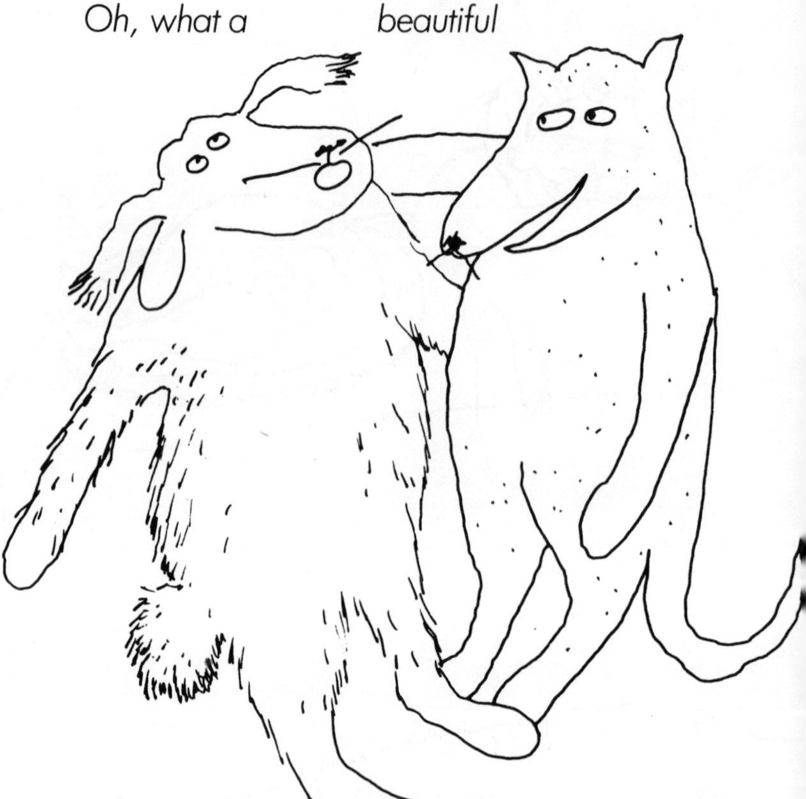
Oh, what a
beautiful

morning!

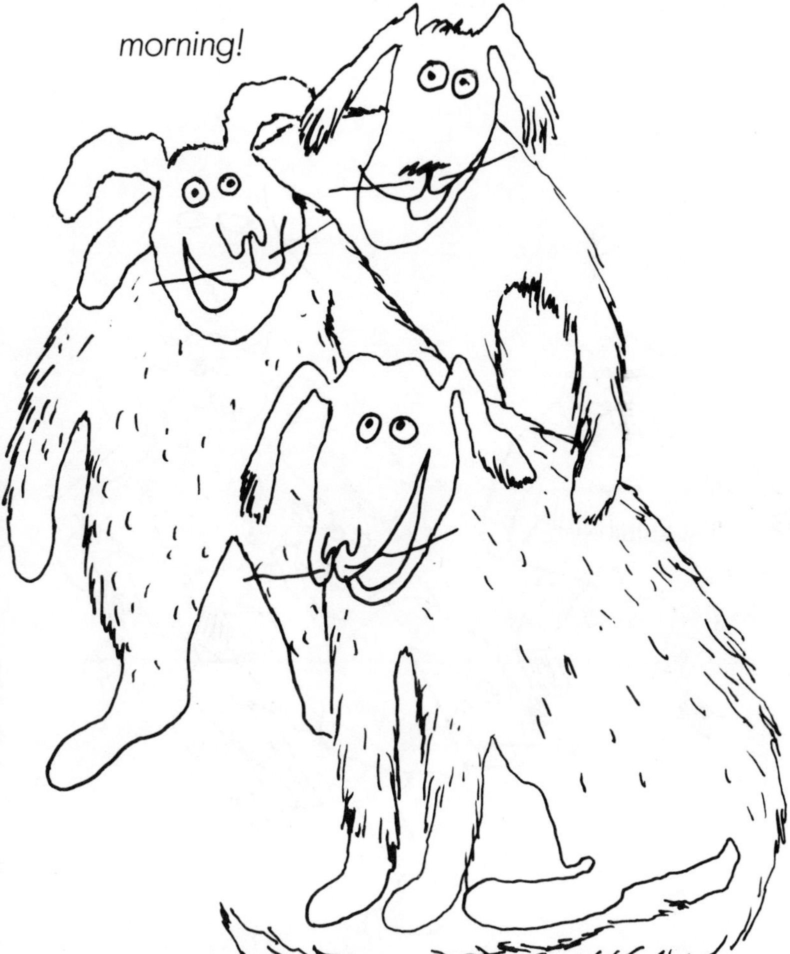

CATS need catnip.

*Hey, kits, how about
a hit of great catnip?*

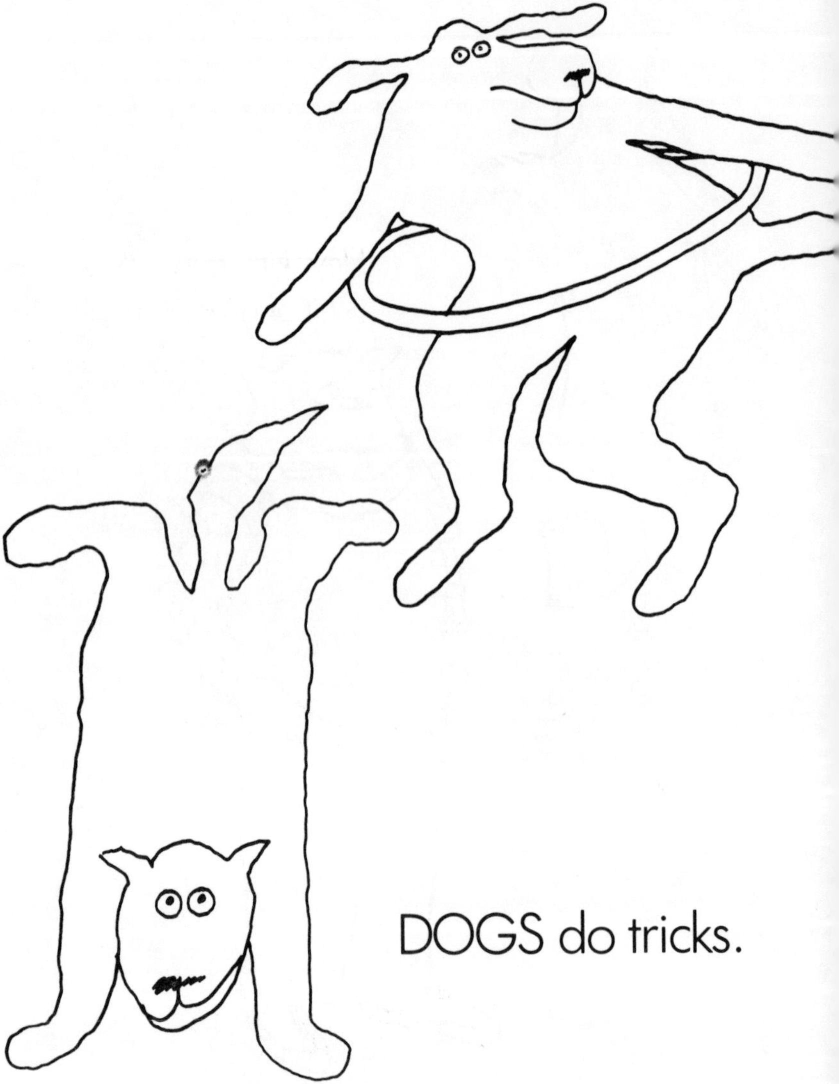

DOGS do tricks.

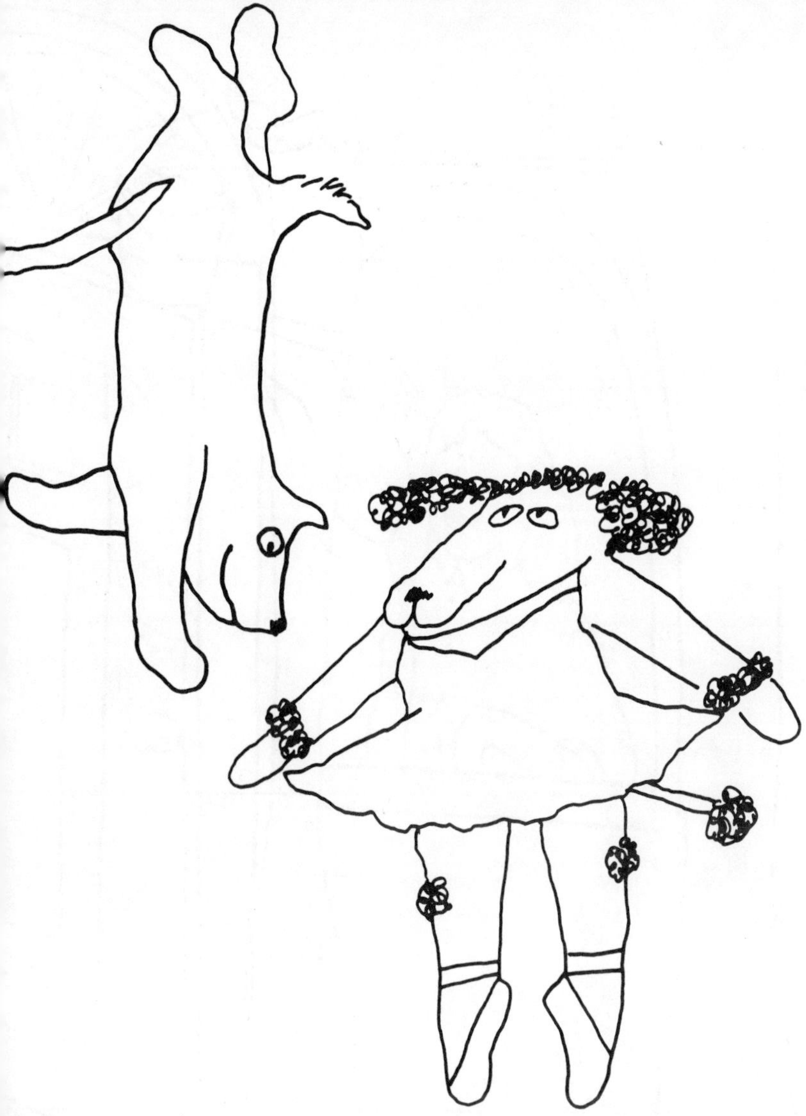

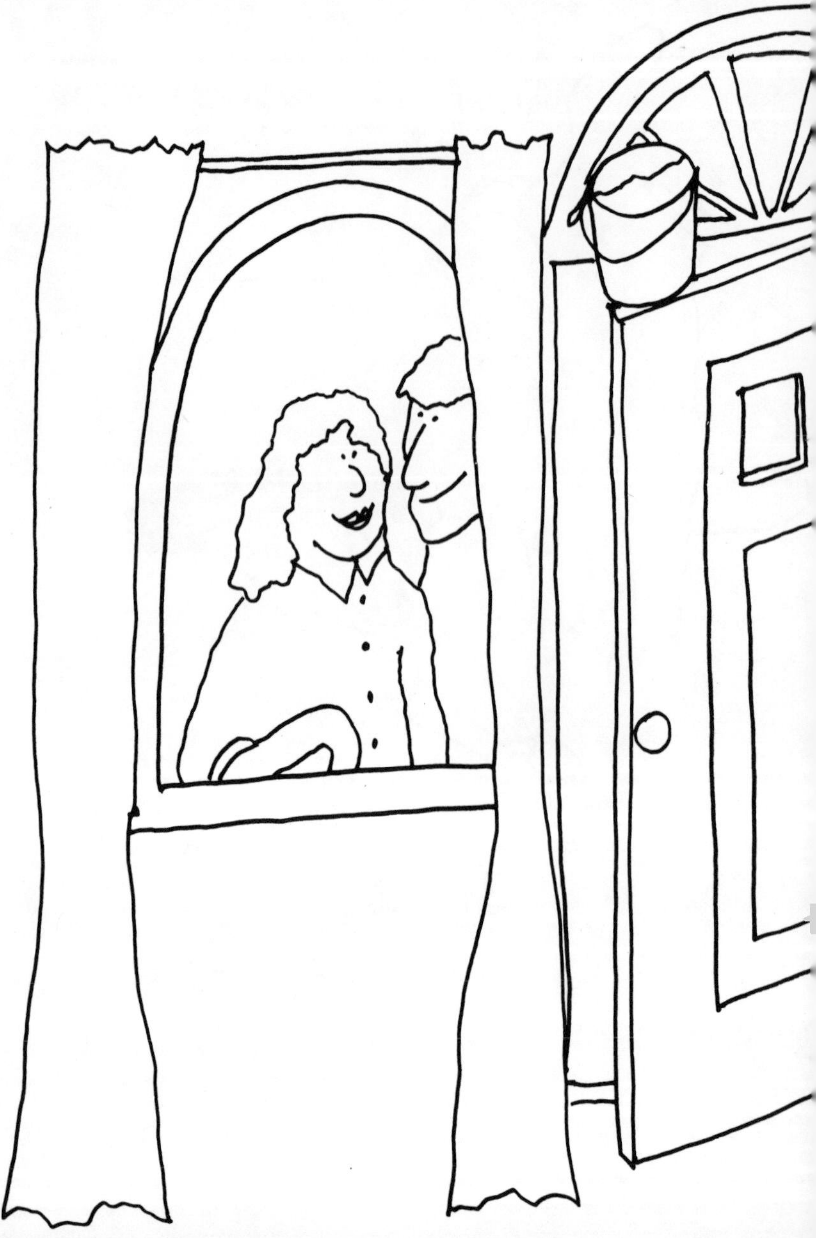

CATS play tricks.

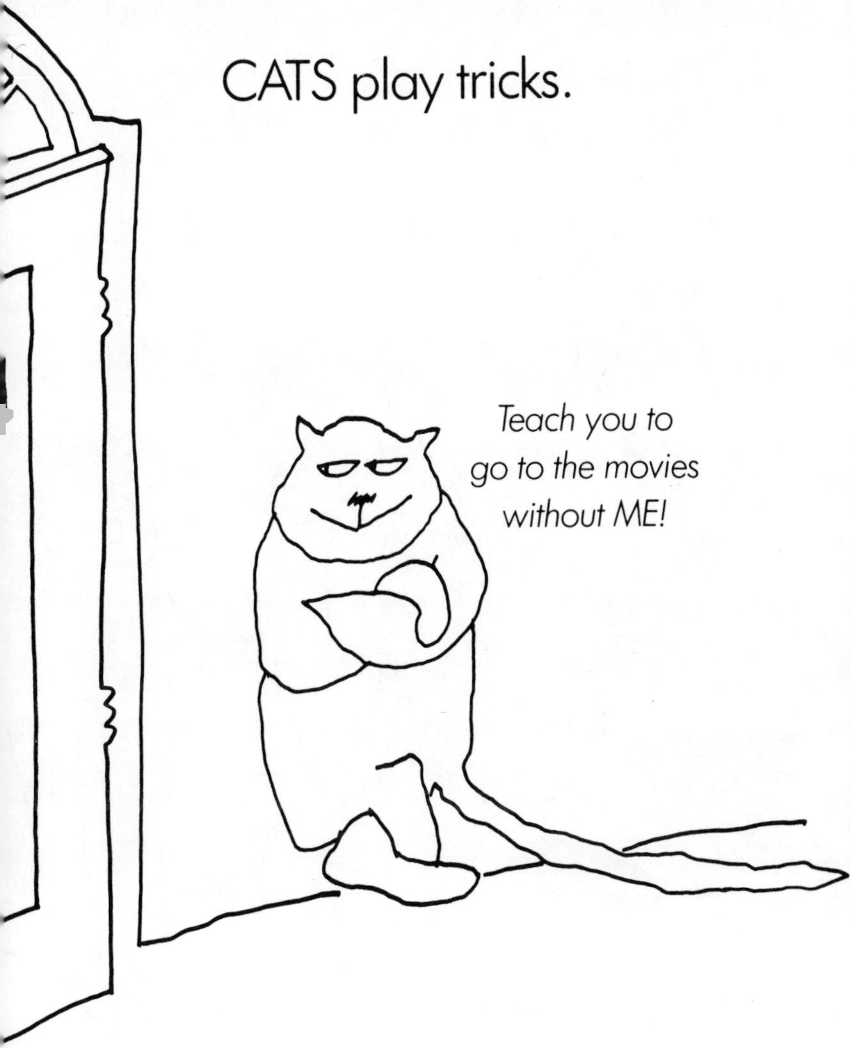
Teach you to go to the movies without ME!

DOGS are content to sound like dogs.

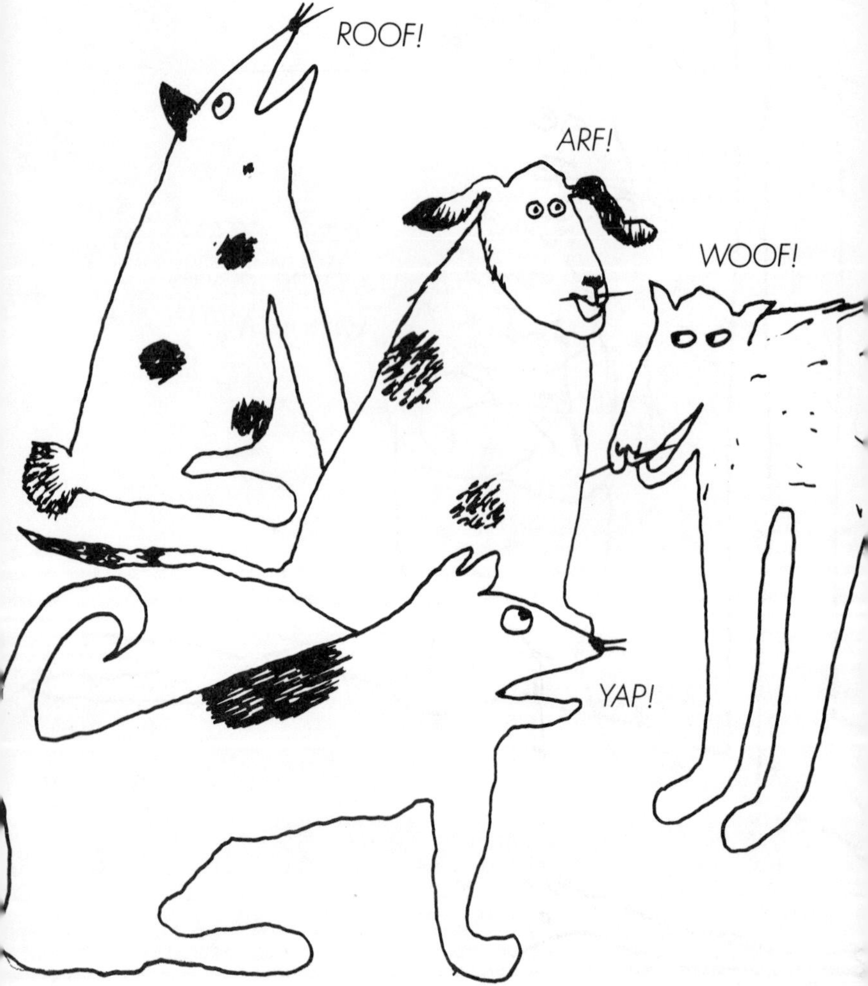
ROOF!
ARF!
WOOF!
YAP!

CATS try to imitate crying babies and jets breaking the sound barrier.

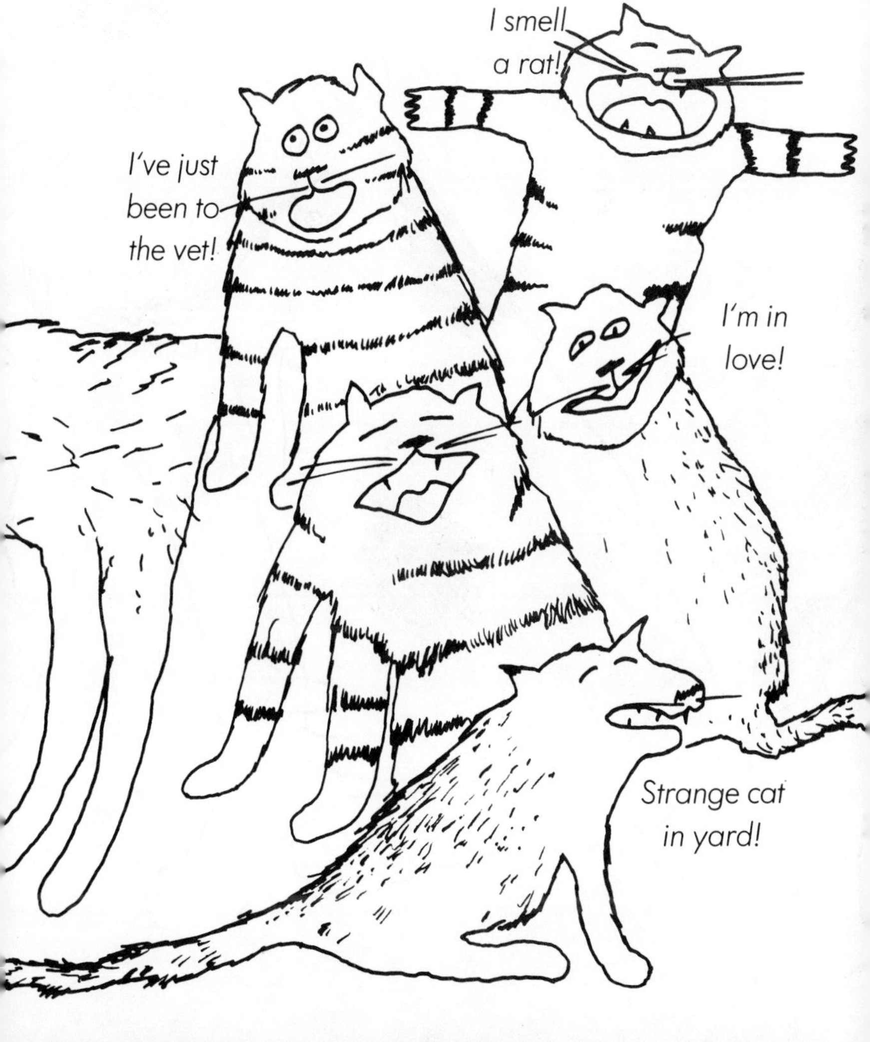
I smell a rat!
I've just been to the vet!
I'm in love!
Strange cat in yard!

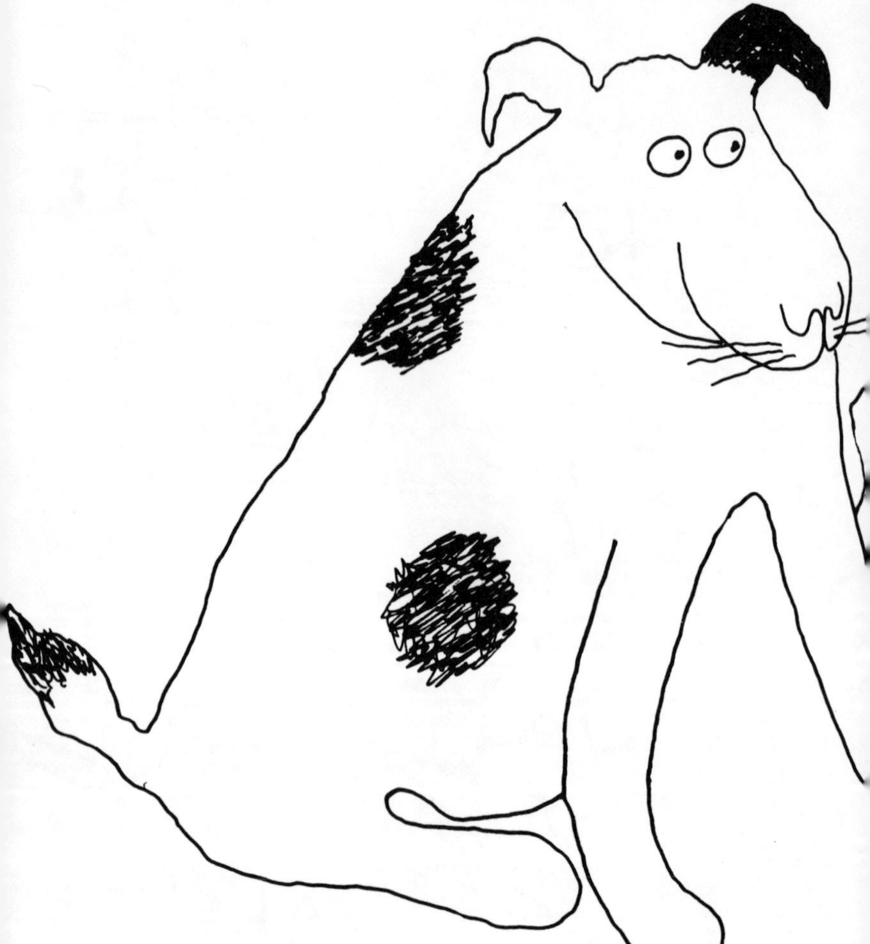

DOG LITTER.

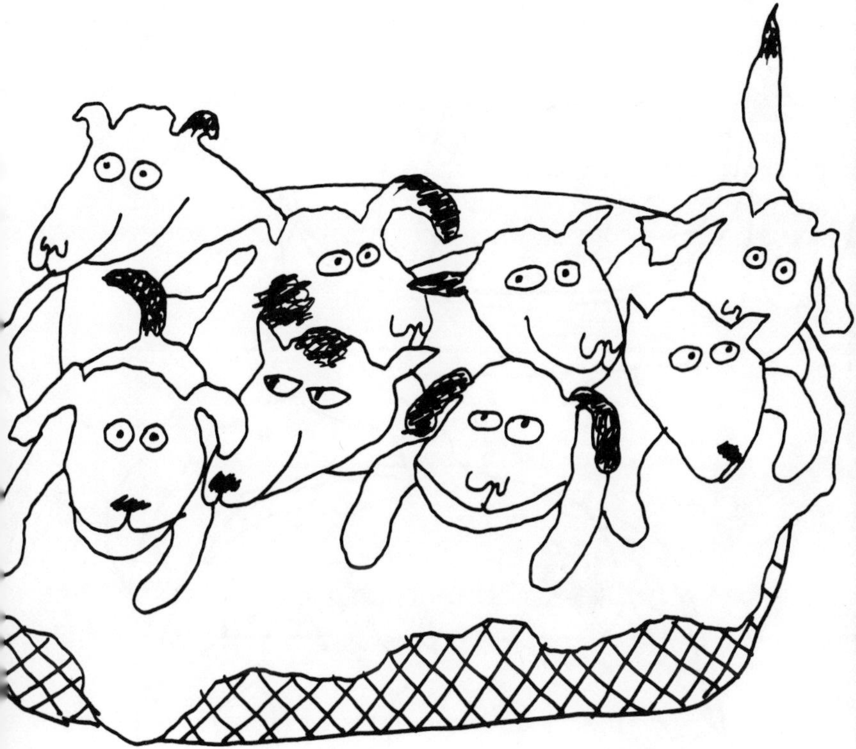

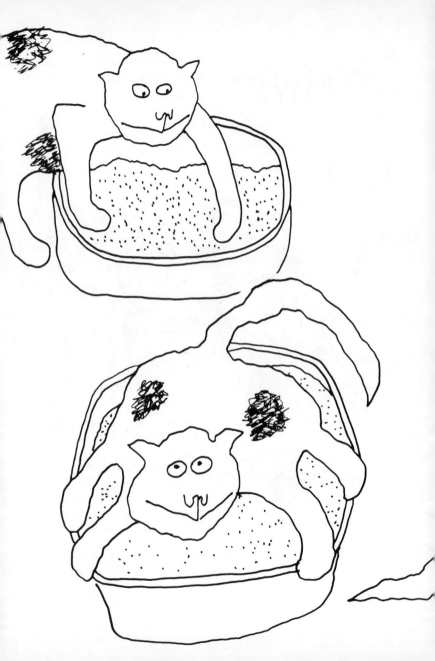

KITTY LITTER.

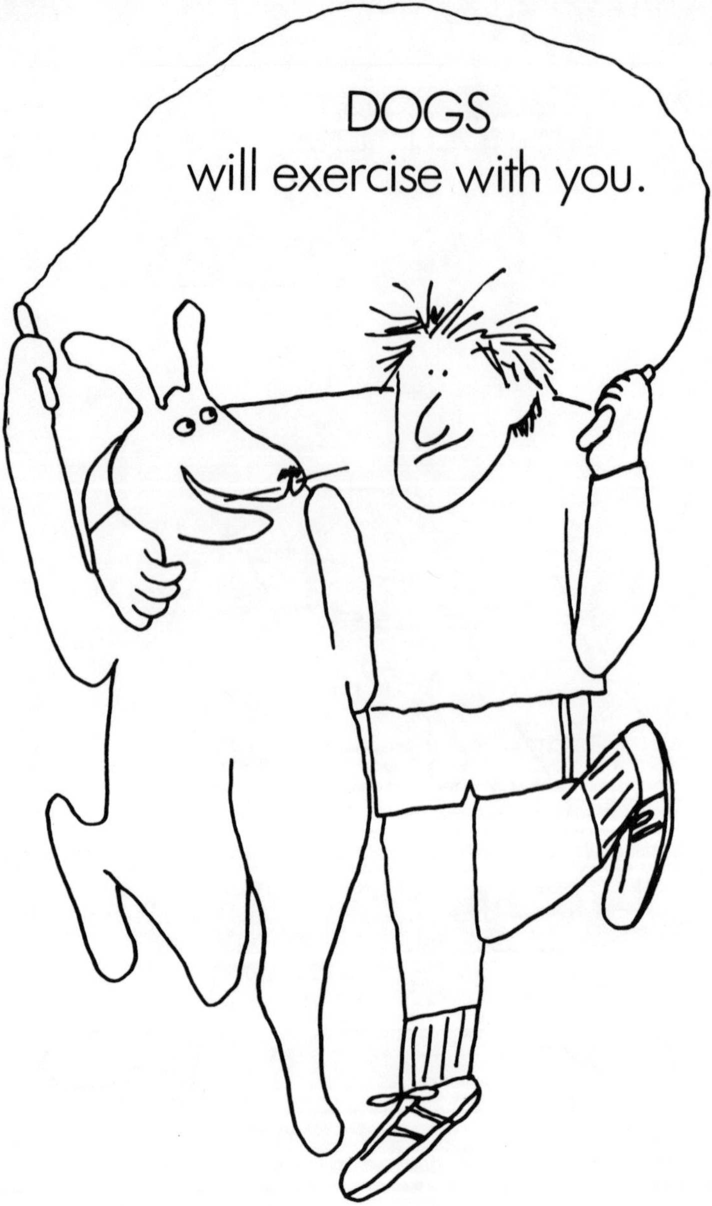
DOGS
will exercise with you.

CATatonic

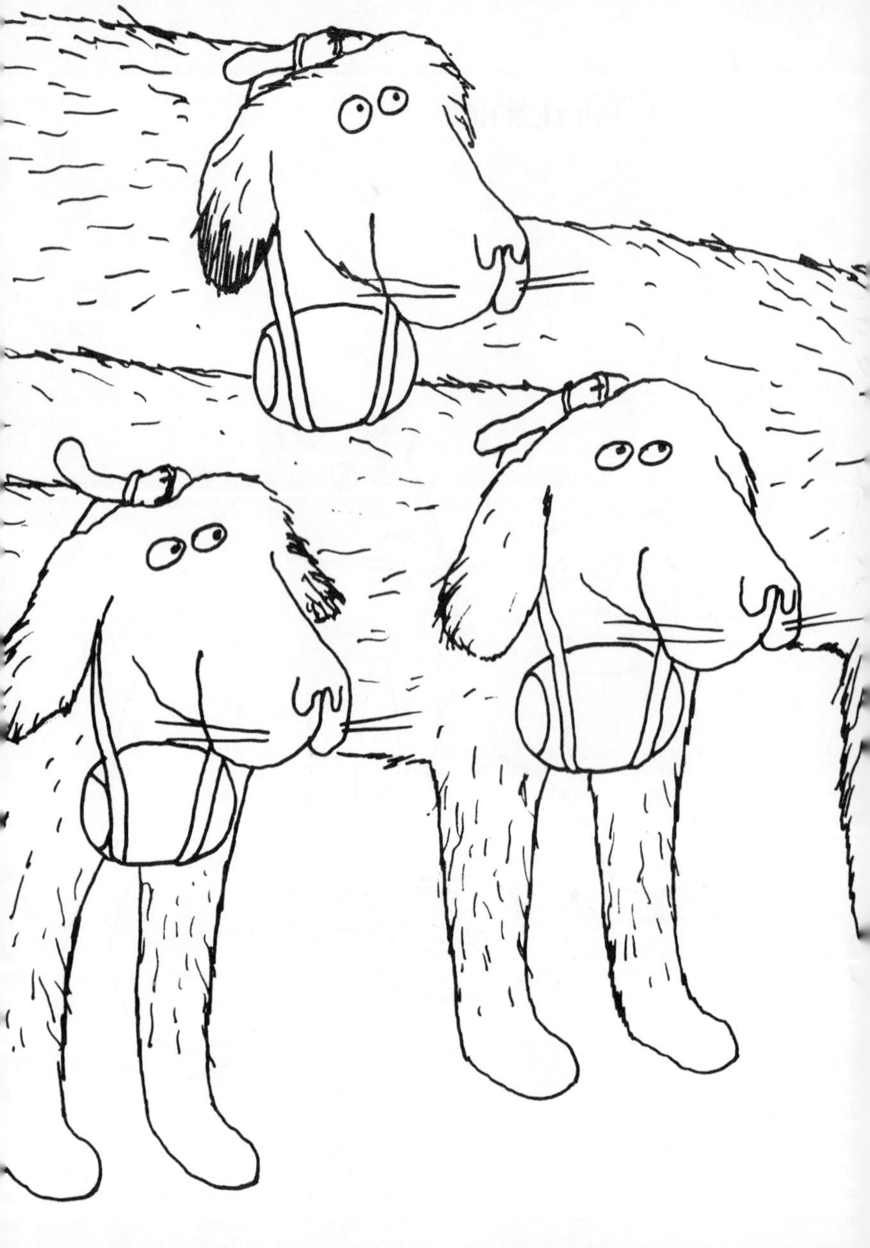

DOGGED

Show us some snow!
Show us a cold person!

Show me a
fire! Show
me a warm person!

CATTY

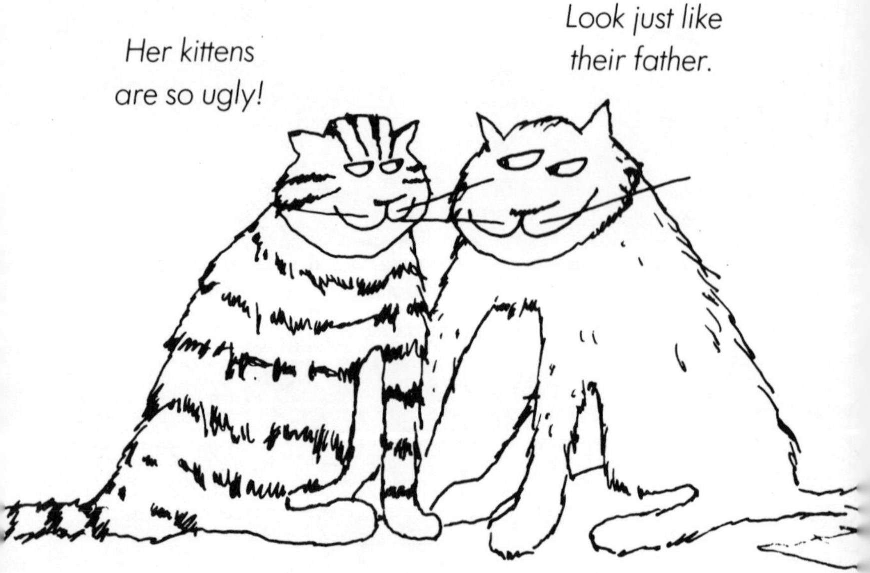
Her kittens
are so ugly!
Look just like
their father.

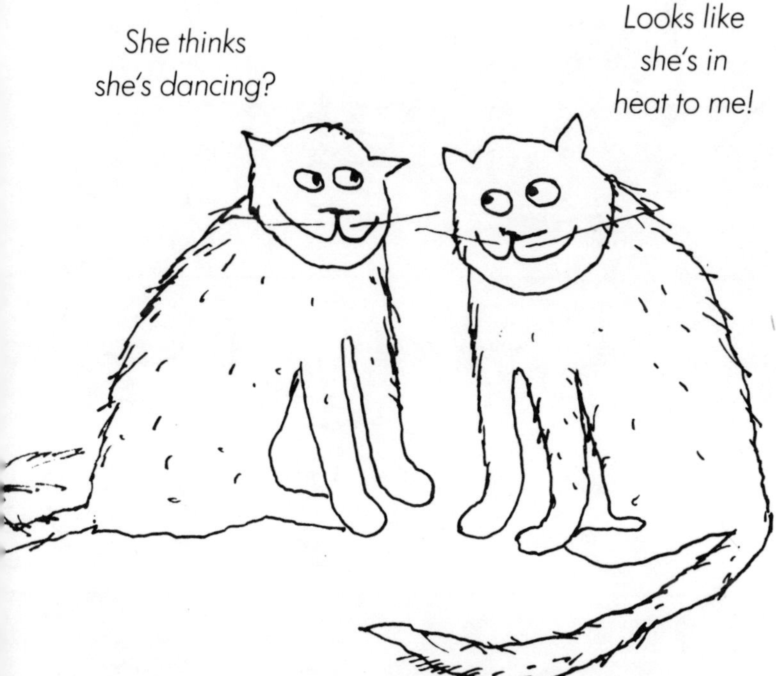
She thinks
she's dancing?
Looks like
she's in
heat to me!

Restaurants send food home for DOGS.

Oh, what a treat —
macaroni!

Soupbone!

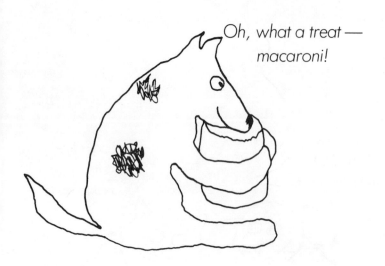

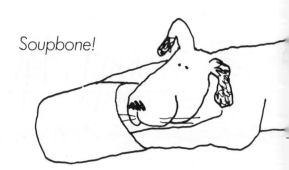

Toast!

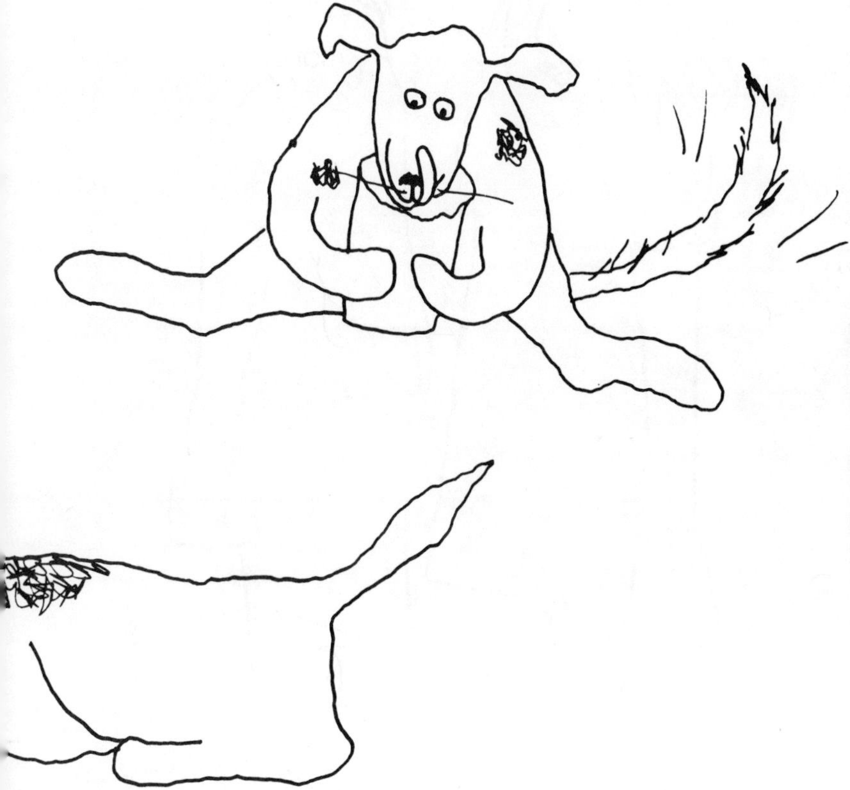

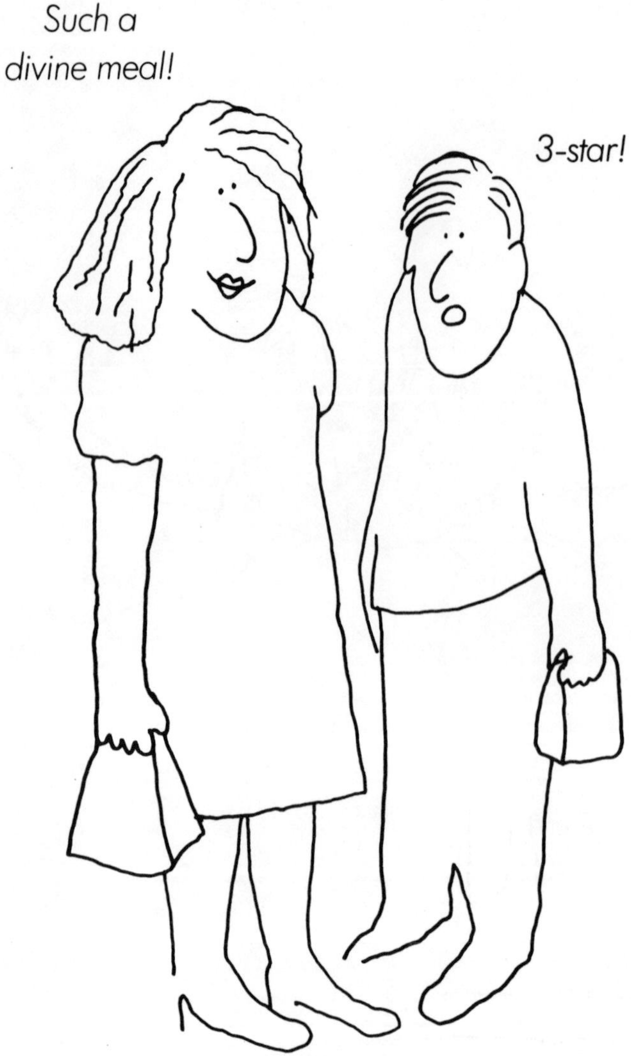
Such a divine meal!
3-star!

There are NO KITTY bags.

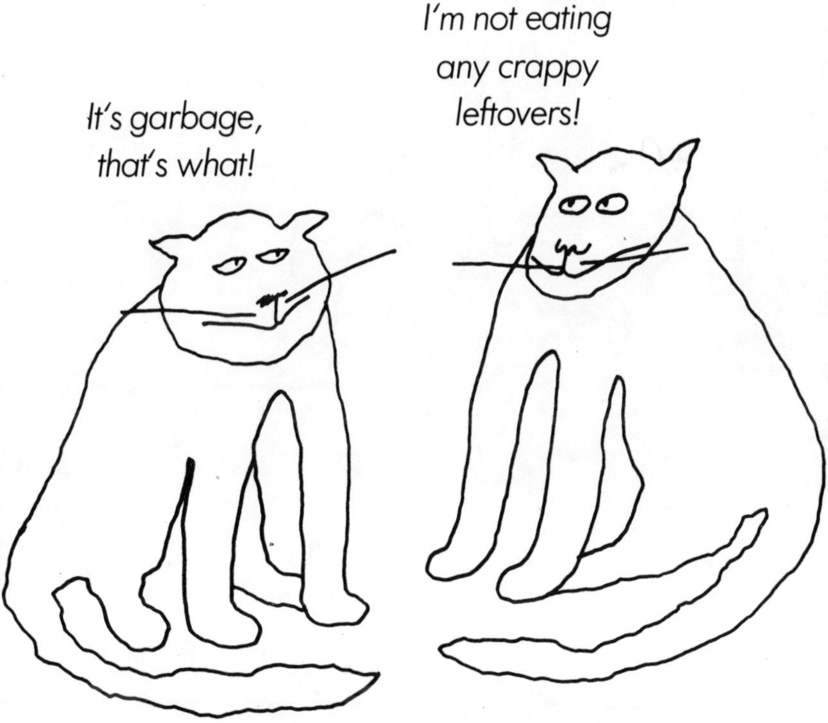
It's garbage,
that's what!
I'm not eating
any crappy
leftovers!

DOGS get along well with most other pets.

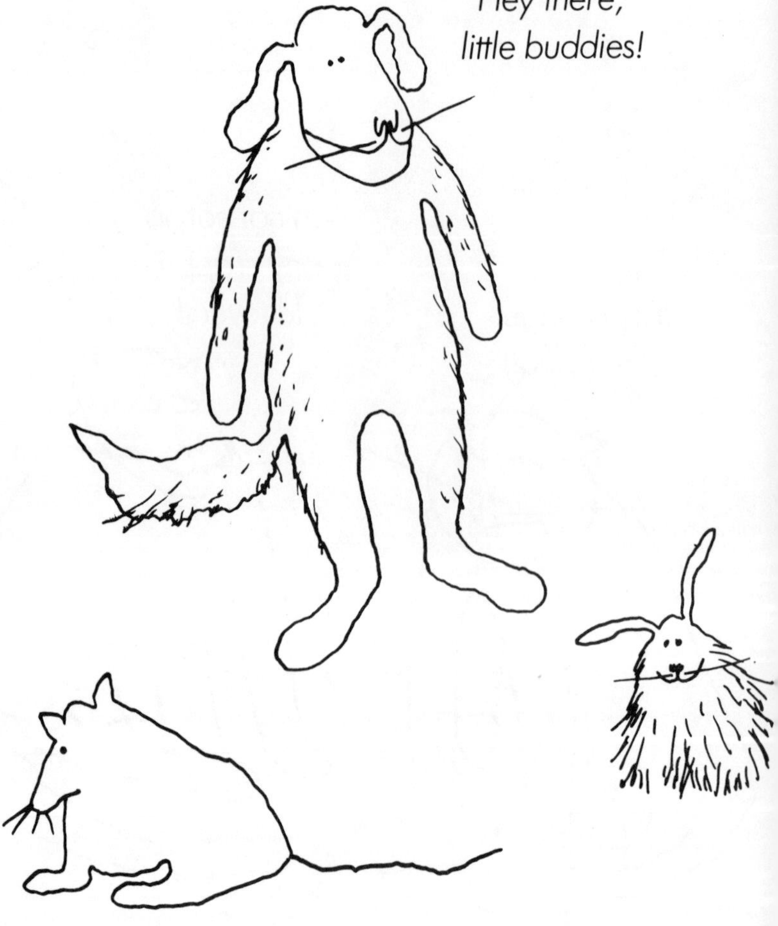
Hey there, little buddies!

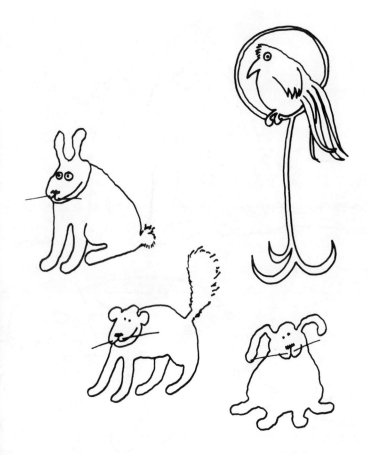

CATS eat other pets.

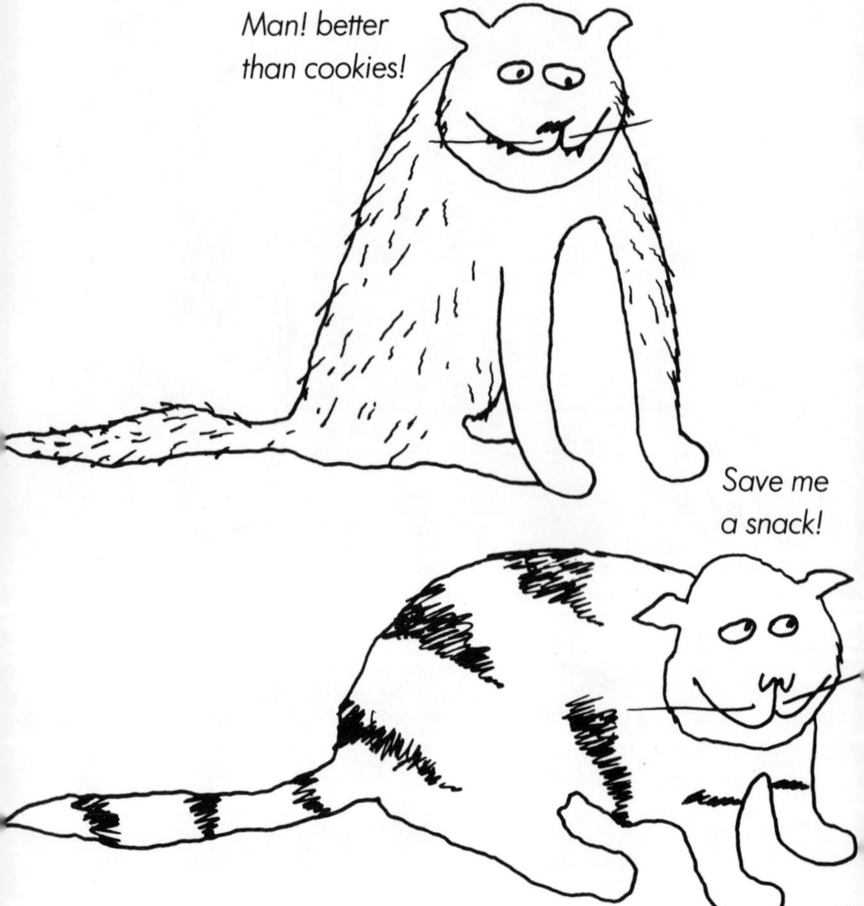
Man! better than cookies!
Save me a snack!

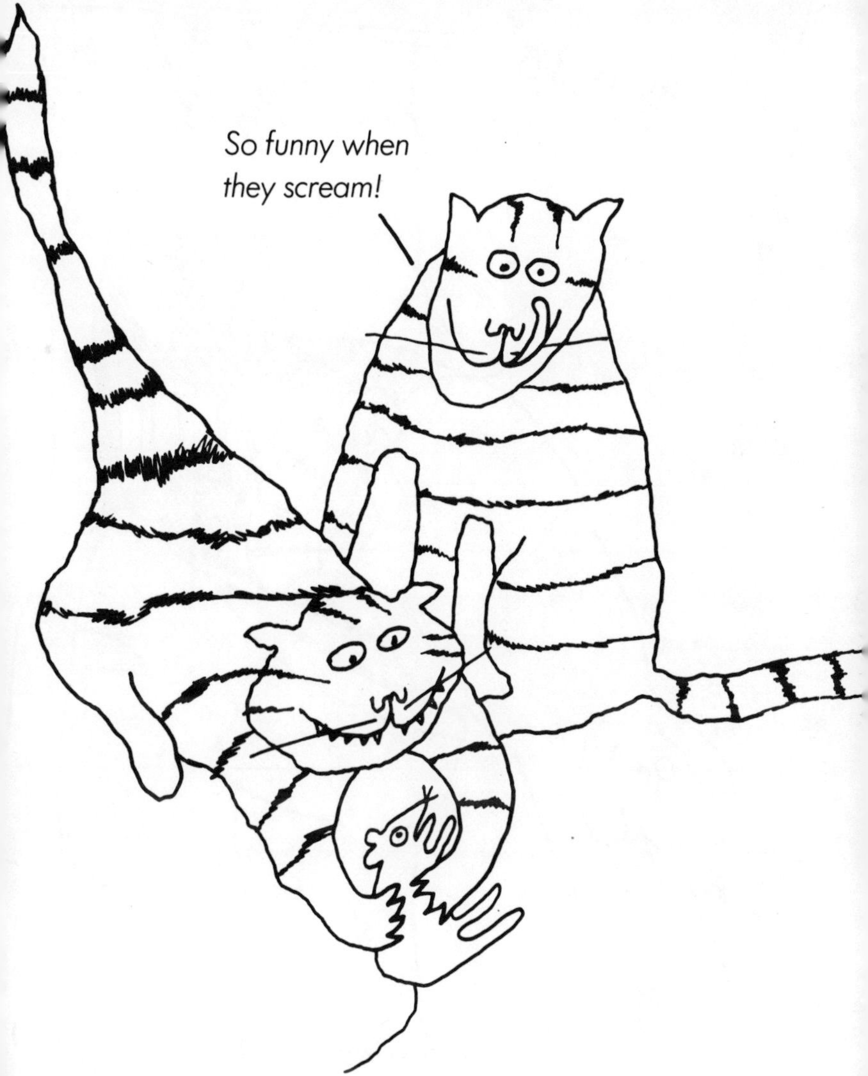
So funny when
they scream!

DOGNAP

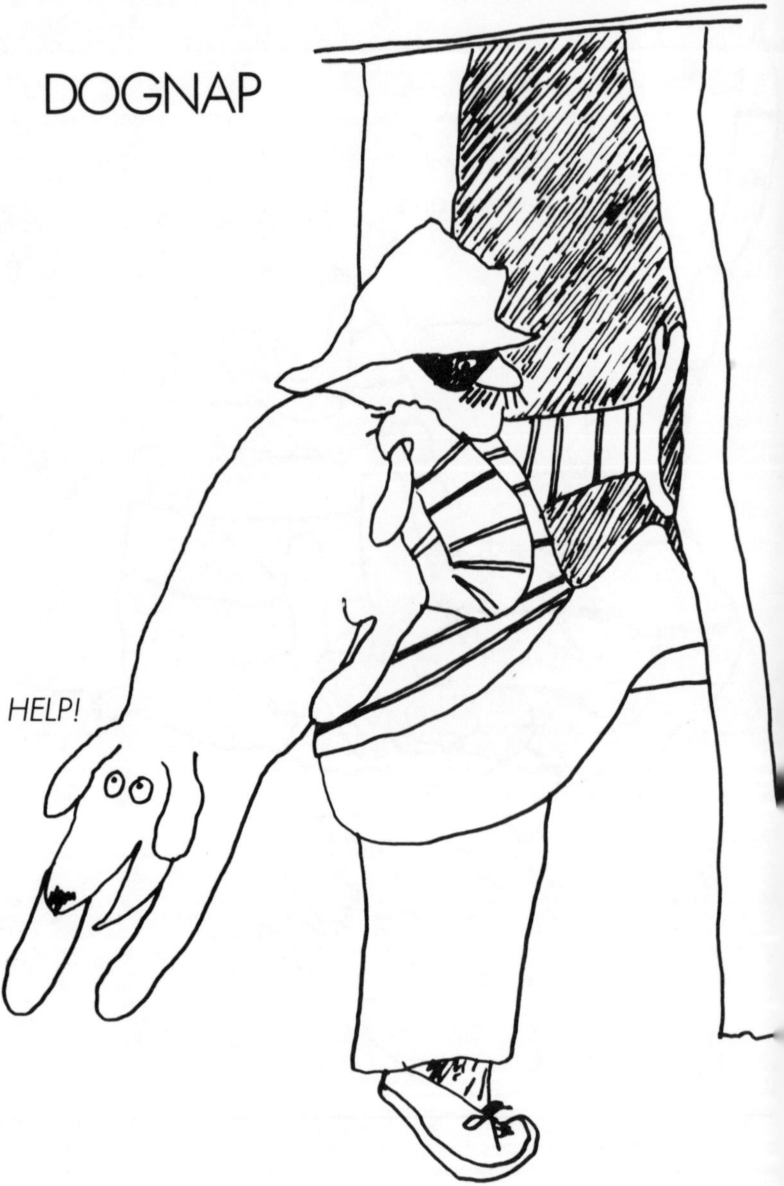
HELP!

CATNAP

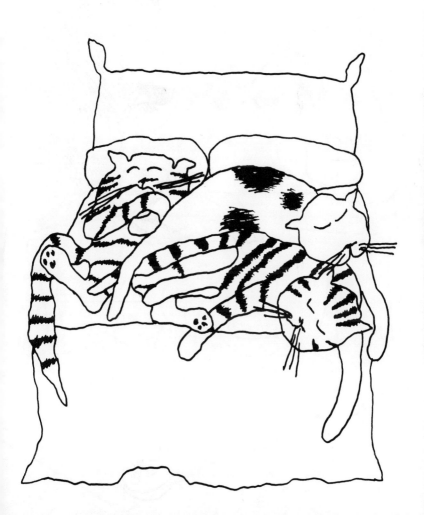

DOGS get haircuts.

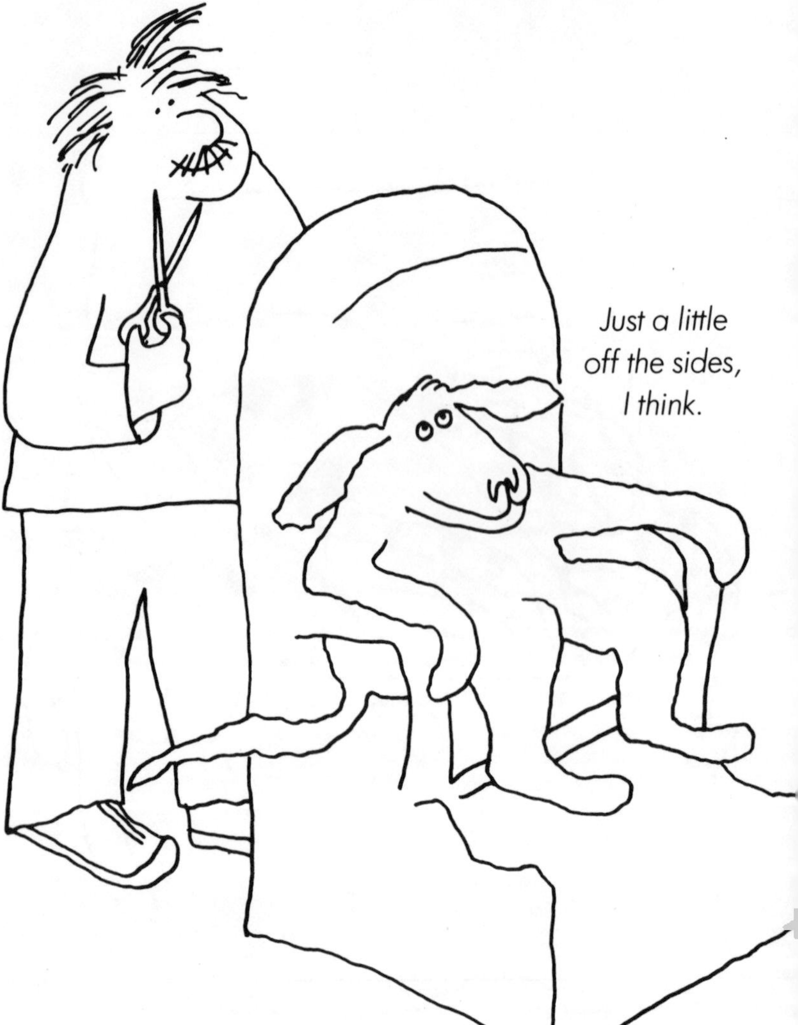
Just a little
off the sides,
I think.

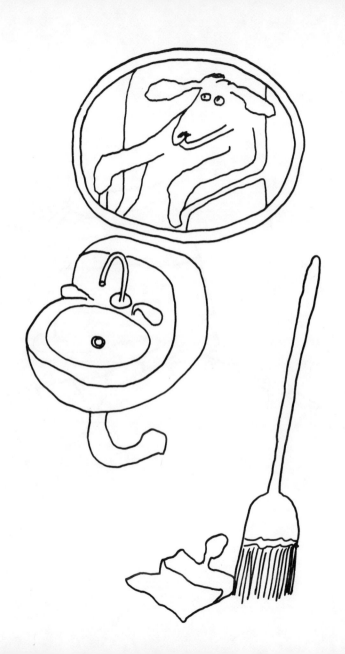

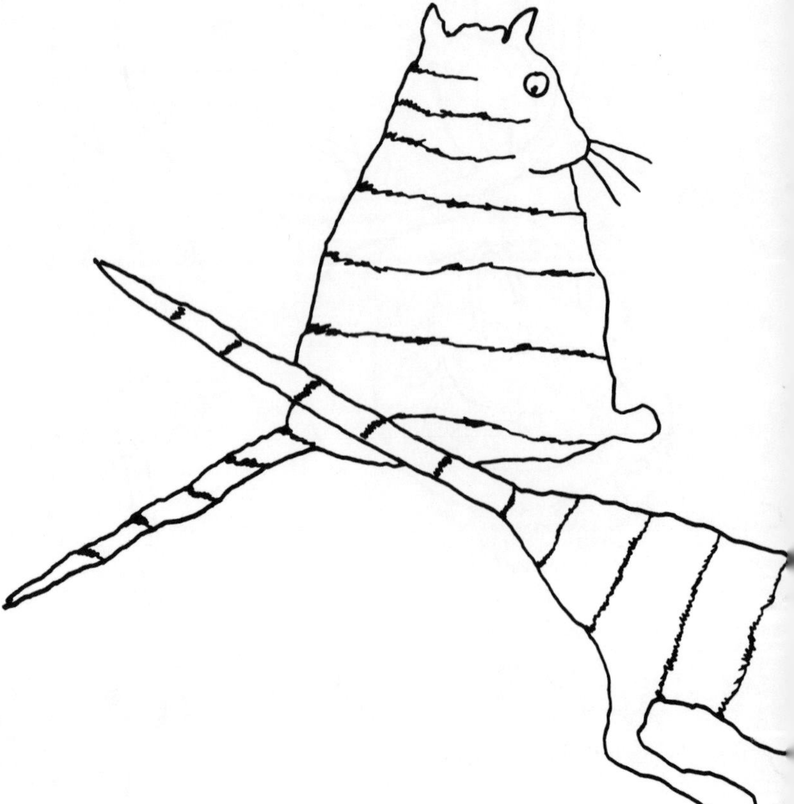

CATS get hairballs.

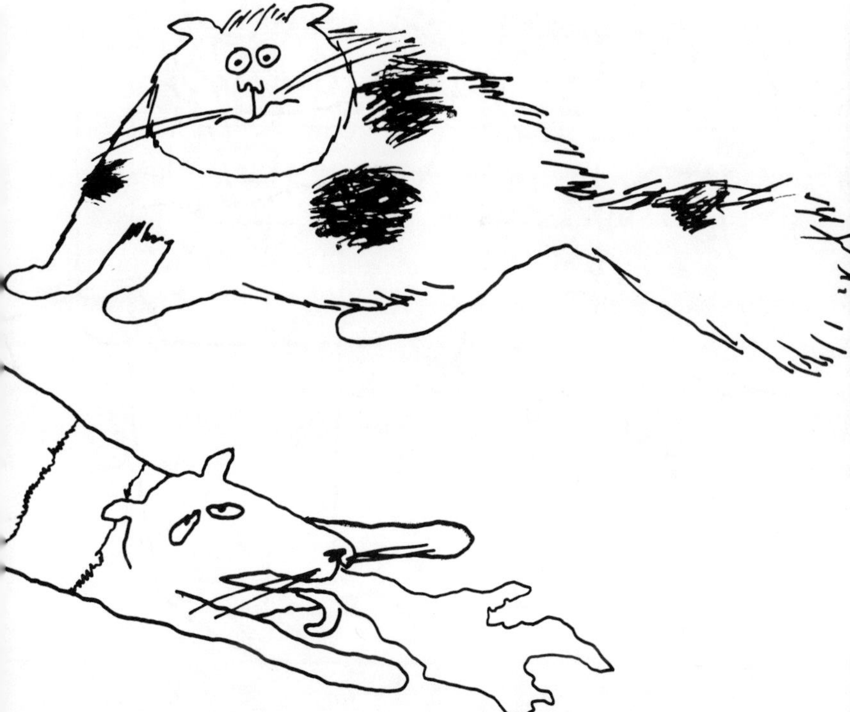

Put on the DOG.

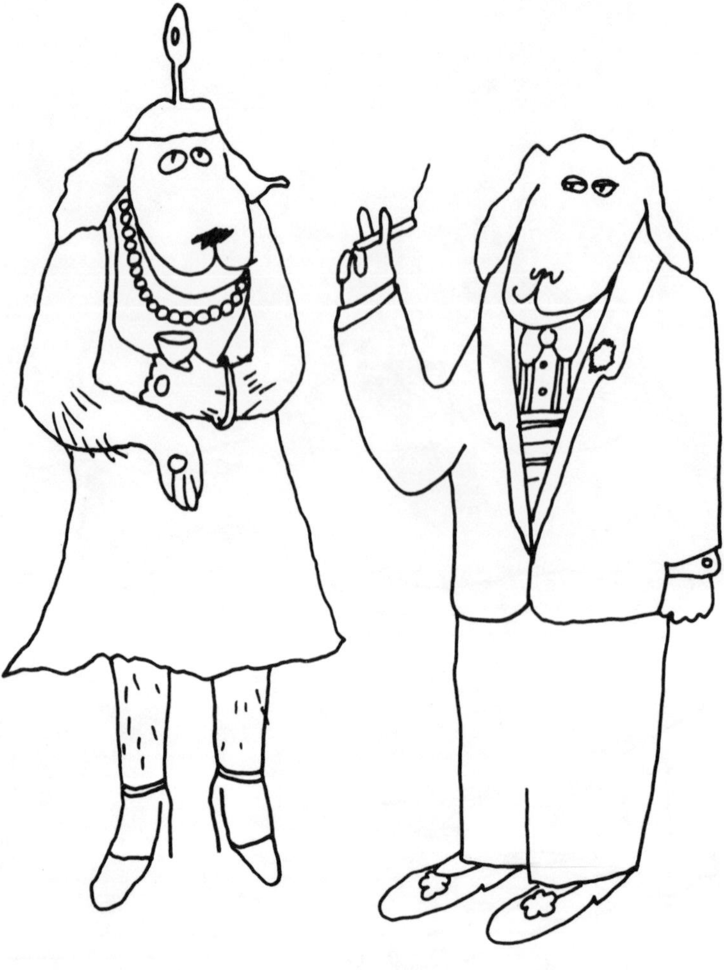

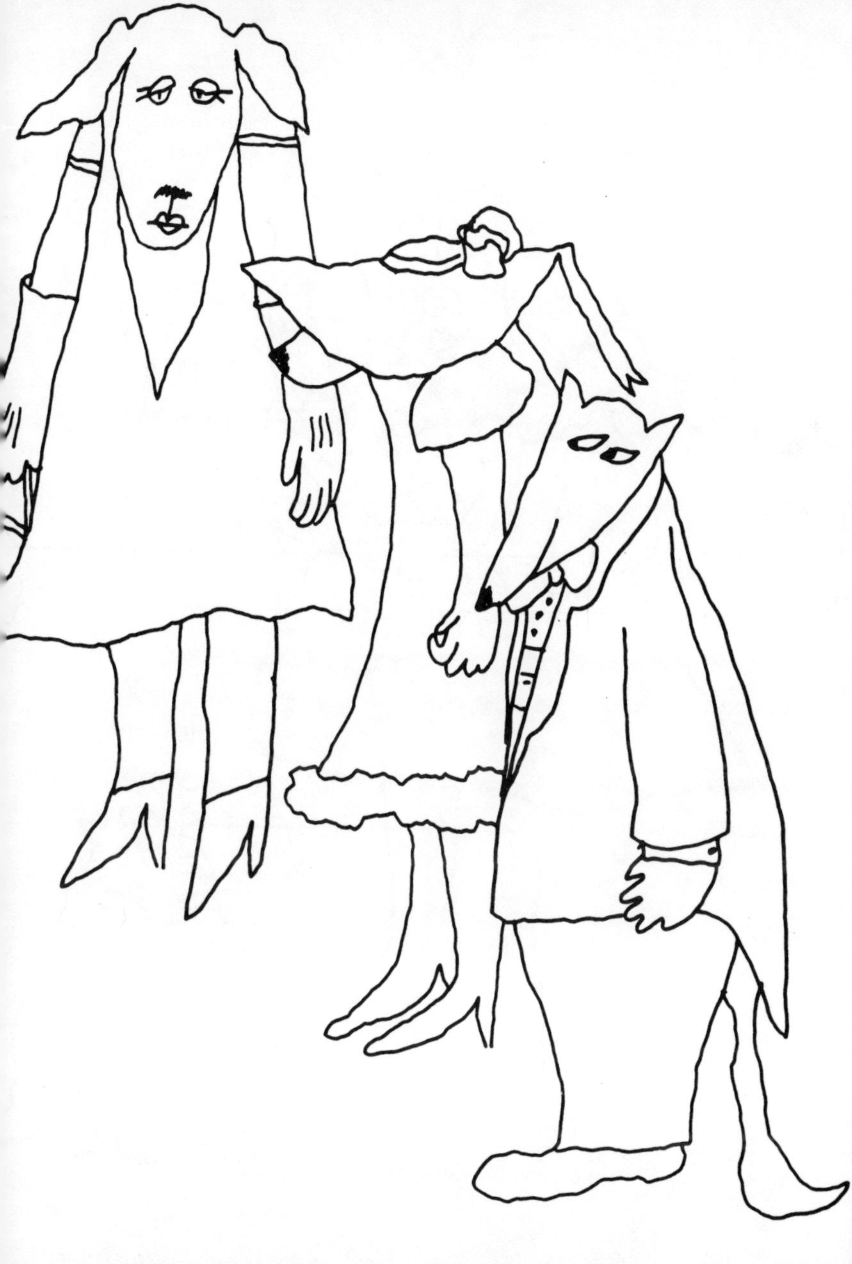

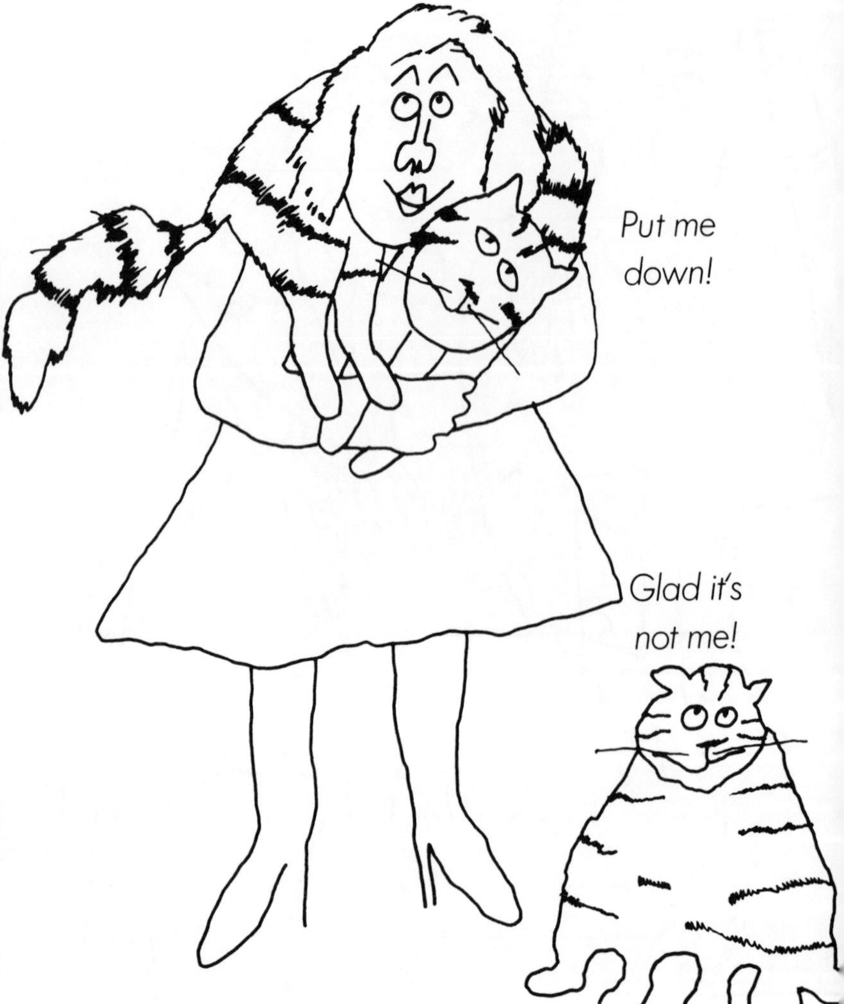
Put me down!
Glad it's not me!

Put on the CAT?

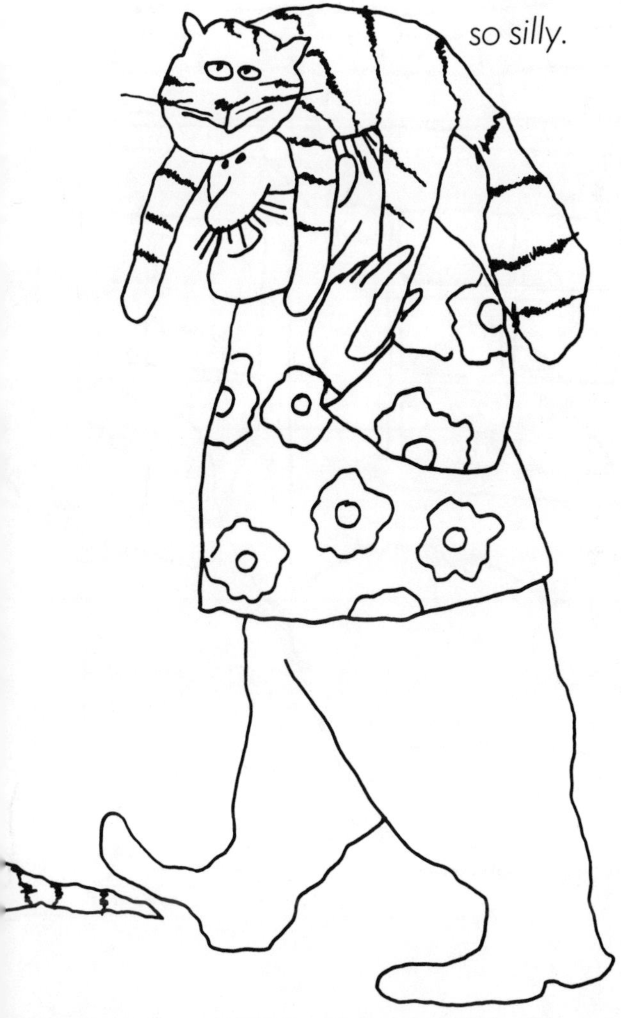
I feel so silly.

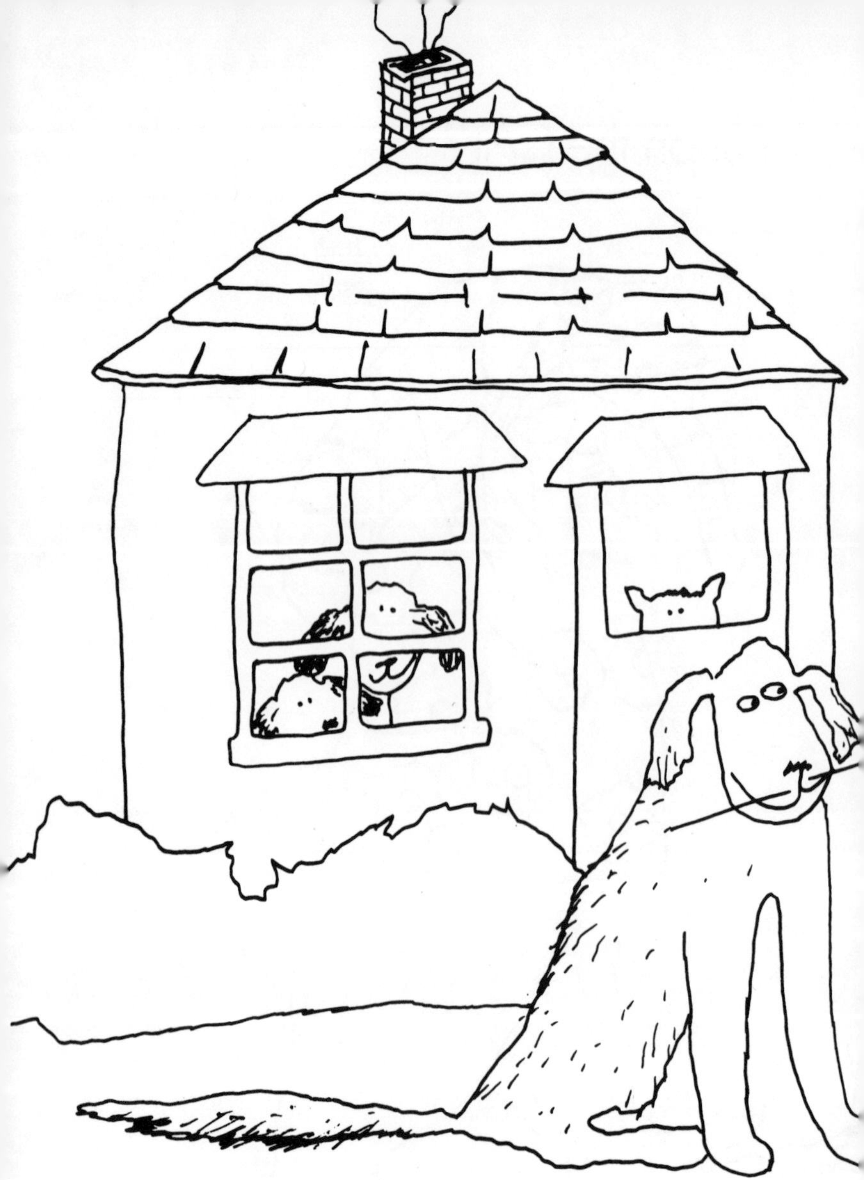

DOGHOUSE

Our lovely decorator home. So All-American!

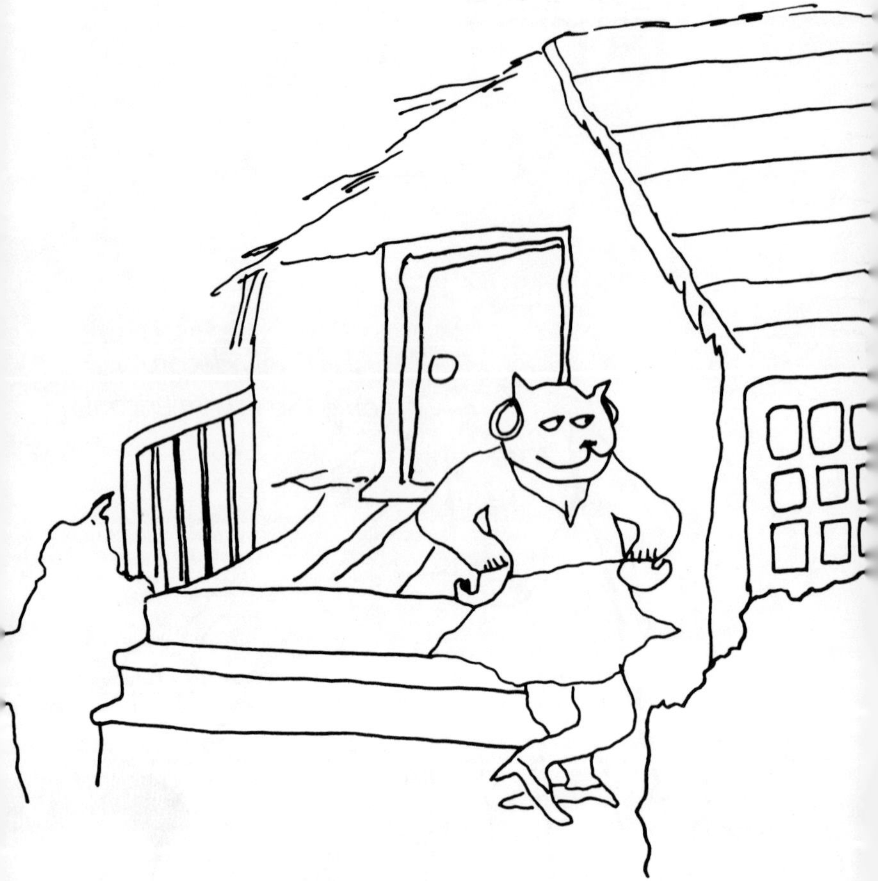

CAT-HOUSE

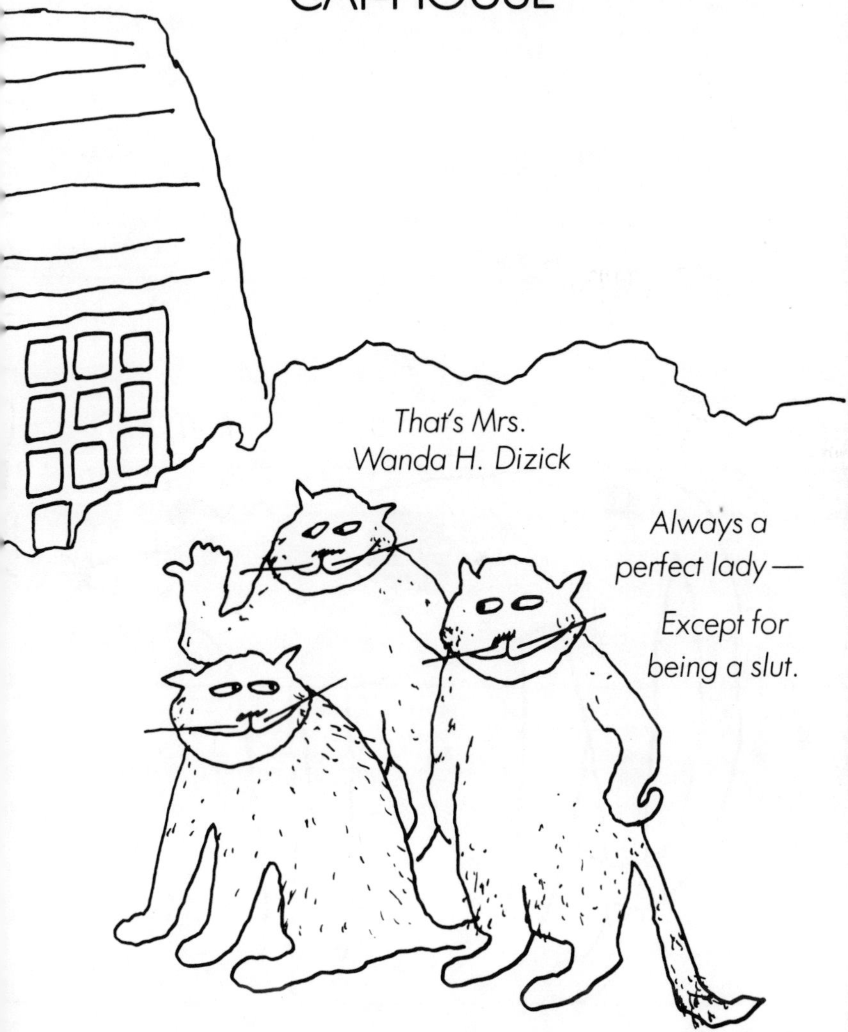
That's Mrs.
Wanda H. Dizick
Always a
perfect lady —
Except for
being a slut.

DOGS know that life is...

Ruff, ruff!

CATS don't think of life, only of themselves. That's why they say...

ME-ow

THE END